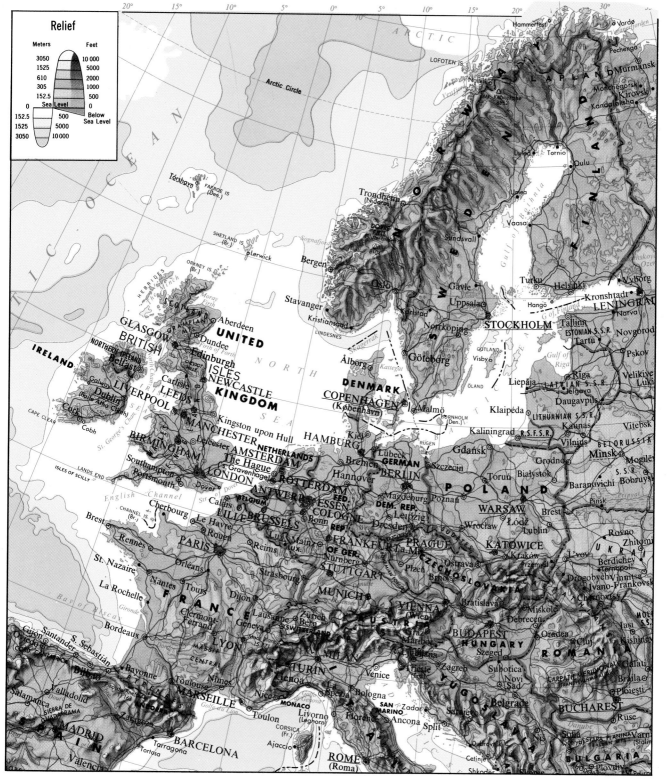

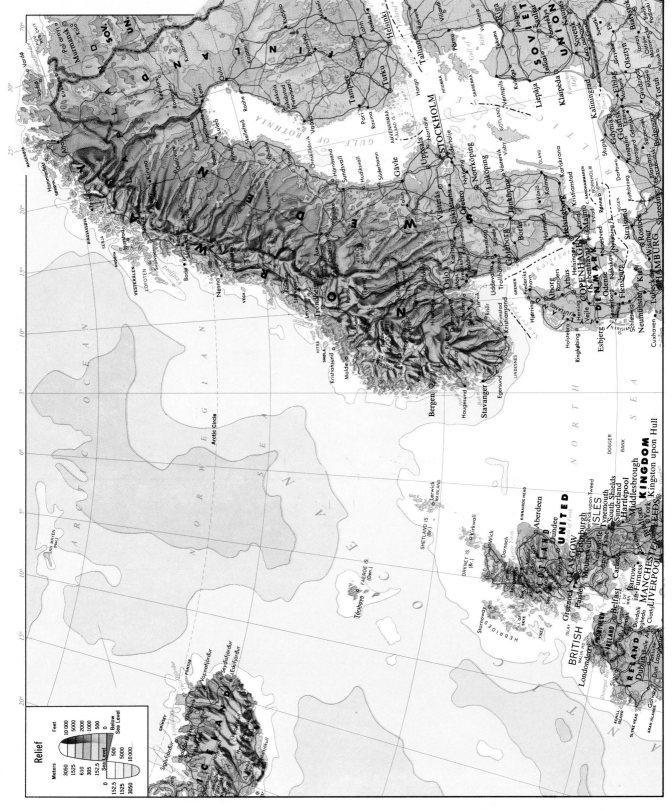

Relief

Meters	Feet
3050	10 000
1525	5000
610	2000
305	1000
152.5	500
0	Sea Level
152.5	500
1525	5000
3050	10 000

Below Sea Level

Scale 1: 10 000 000; one inch to 160 miles. Conic Projection

Elevations and depressions are given in feet

Enchantment of the World

SWEDEN

By Martin Hintz

Consultant: Ingrid Claréus, M.A., Instructor, Department of Scandinavian Studies, The University of Wisconsin, Madison, Wisconsin

Consultant for Reading: Robert L. Hillerich, Ph.D., Bowling Green University, Bowling Green, Ohio

 CHILDRENS PRESS ®

CHICAGO

Landscape of central Sweden

Enchantment of the World: Sweden is dedicated to the peace-loving spirit of all Swedes, especially to that of Dag Hammarskjöld.

Library of Congress Cataloging in Publication Data

Hintz, Martin.
  Sweden.

  (Enchantment of the world)
  Includes index.
  Summary: An introduction to the geography, history, economy, government, people, and culture of Sweden.
  1. Sweden—Description and travel—1981-
Juvenile literature.   2. Sweden—Social life and customs—
—Juvenile literature. [1. Sweden] I. Title.
II. Series.
DL619.5.H56 1985   948.5   85-2643
ISBN 0-516-02788-3   AACR2

Picture Acknowledgments
Shostal Associates: Hubertus Kanus: Page 4; William L. Hamilton: Page 109 (right)
Roloc Color Slides: Cover, Pages 5, 25 (right), 34, 79 (right), 82, 105
Hillstrom Stock Photo: © Mary Ann Brockman: Pages 6, 14, 19 (2 photos), 24, 25 (left), 26, 27, 66 (2 photos), 73 (right); © 1985 Art Brown: Pages 11 (right), 98 (bottom); Art Brown Collection: Pages 52 (center), 94; © Jean Damish, Page 12; © Len Kaufman: Pages 40 (bottom), 97 (2 photos), 104; © Eugene G. Schulz: Pages 69, 84, 108, 109 (left); © Dr. Hans Kramarz: Page 70 (top); © E.J. Flickinger: Page 96

The Swedish Institute: Chad Ehlers: Pages 9, 49 (left), 90, 103; Courtesy of the Volvo BM Company: Page 23; Courtesy of the Siemens-Elema Company: Page 49 (right); Courtesy of the LKAB Company, Page 67
Journalism Services/FTP: © Wolfgang Timmermann: Pages 8, 28 (top), 32, 68, 80, 81
Historical Pictures Service, Chicago: Pages 11 (left), 30, 31, 33, 35, 36, 37, 39, 52 (left & right), 53 (left), 79 (left & center), 93 (2 photos)
Bob & Ira Spring, Edmonds, Washington: Pages 15, 17, 18, 50, 60 (top), 61 (top left), 63, 64 (right), 70 (bottom), 75, 77, 86 (top), 98 (top), 100
Chip and Rosa Maria Peterson: Page 16; © Margareta Bayer: Pages 20, 51, 64 (left)
Photo Researchers, Inc.: Paolo Koch: Page 21; © F. Gohier 1983: Page 76 (2 photos)
Virginia Grimes: Pages 22 (left), 59 (left), 60 (bottom), 73 (left), 74, 101
Tom Stack & Associates: © Dale Jorgenson: Pages 22 (right), 38
Nawrocki Stock Photo: © D. Variajokis: Page 28 (bottom left)
Jerome Wyckoff: Page 28 (bottom right)
Root Resources: © Roger J. Naser: Pages 40 (top), 86 (bottom); © W. Helfrich: Page 78
AP/World Wide Photos: Page 43
UPI Photo: Page 53 (right)
Colour Library International: Page 89; Nick Meers: Pages 46, 54, 57, 58, 59 (right), 61 (top right & bottom)
Charles R. Stone: Pages 83, 95
The Marilyn Gartman Agency: © David Seman: Page 102
Len W. Meents: Maps on pages 15, 57, 63, 67, 68
Courtesy Flag Research Center, Winchester, Massachusetts 01890: Flag on back cover
Cover: View of Stockholm's Old Town

*Folk
costume*

TABLE OF CONTENTS

Chapter 1

THE KINGDOM

OF THE TREES

Sweden seems to be awash with trees. Everywhere, spiky green pines push toward the sun. Long branches clutch at the clouds like fingers trying to scale the sky. Acres and acres and acres of trees—somebody once said there were fifty-one billion trees in Sweden. Nobody has taken the time to count, but who's to disagree?

The trees have made and have shaped Sweden. The forests are deep, silent, and brooding; they seem to be waiting and watching for something to happen. Moss covers the ground and lichens cover rocks that are said to be trolls turned to stone. Light filters through overhead branches, gently bathing a scene in lush richness. In the winter, deep snows soften the edges of boulders with a chilly blanket.

Amid the thick groves are 96,000 lakes. (Nobody has taken the time to count these either.) That figure takes in the larger bodies of crystal clear water, but not every single pond and puddle.

Somewhere out in that spread of water and wood are eight million people. Outside the bustling cities, the Swedes are spread

The island of Gotland in the Baltic Sea is a popular vacation spot.

thinly across the land. Another eight million citizens could easily be tucked away in that expanse. But Swedes don't like to be crowded. There is plenty of room for everyone.

The sprawling land with all the greenery has molded an independent spirit. This might sound contradictory, because the Swedish government looks after its citizens from birth to death. Cities are crowded, yet full of tall apartment buildings. ''We don't like to shovel sidewalks,'' jokes one Swede who lives in a towering apartment house.

Yet ordinary Swedes are willing to live in crowded towns if they can get away for a while, to camp in the forests or spend time in wilderness cabins. Weekends and summers are escape times to relax the body and clear the mind. These respites, their retreat into the soothing comfort of the woods, help the Swedish family move through the rest of the year.

Most Swedes lead a comfortable life.

THE GOOD LIFE

The Swedes are happy that they have found what they consider the Good Life. They may not be living in luxury, but they are very comfortable. Their standard of living is among the highest in Europe. The Swedes are well dressed and their houses are crammed with appliances. They often have two cars and some homes have several television sets.

This did not come easily. The Swedes have had to work very hard for the Good Life. The Industrial Revolution reached Sweden late, but the country quickly seized on the new techniques of manufacturing. The industrious Swedes are now famous for shipbuilding, logging, mining, crystal and glassmaking, and other ventures.

Sweden was able to develop without much outside interference, unlike many of her European neighbors. She was very powerful in the seventeenth and eighteenth centuries and fought many wars outside her territories. Nobody wanted to tackle Sweden on her own soil, so the country was never ravaged by foreign armies. After the Swedes were finally defeated as a major military power, the rest of Europe left her alone. Now, Sweden is strong again— but in another way. She is one of the major financial and banking countries in the world.

And, more important, Sweden is neutral. For more than 150 years she has stayed out of war. She can send her diplomats almost anywhere to help peacemaking efforts because other nations respect her honesty and fairness.

Two examples of these spirited public servants are Count Folke Bernadotte, who was the chief United Nations representative in Palestine in the 1940s, and Dag Hammarskjöld, United Nations secretary general in the 1960s. Being a peacemaker can be a rough job, with many perils. Bernadotte was assassinated by terrorists and Hammarskjöld was killed in a plane crash in Africa. Yet still the Swedes remain in the forefront of those working for peace in an unfriendly world.

A DELICATE BALANCE

Perhaps the serenity of the forests soothes the Swedish heart and the mind. Nothing seems more foolish than war, say the Swedes, after hiking through the forests and enjoying their calm and quiet.

Sweden is attempting to find a delicate balance between private wants and public needs. Swedes are asking many questions. How

Dag Hammarskjöld (left), secretary general of the United Nations, tried to assure the future of all young people.

does a country make the most of its resources, yet keep the environment clean and open? How does a country build enough housing to shelter its growing population, without crowding everyone? How are industries maintained so that everyone is assured of a good job? they ask.

Swedes are basically quiet people. Don't try to plunge into a friendship with a Swede. "One step at a time" is the honored motto. But once you have made a Swedish friend, that friendship is set forever.

Swedish young people look to the future with the same wonder as youths elsewhere in the world. They also have the same streak of rebellion in them. They don't tend to dwell on their Good Life, but enjoy traveling, helping others, and meeting new challenges.

It's their eagerness to get out and to do things that continues to make Sweden a true "Land of Enchantment."

The northern border area near Norway is mountainous.

Chapter 2

PRELUDE TO SWEDEN

Sweden, the fourth largest country in Europe, is shaped somewhat like a herring diving into the Baltic Sea from the top of the world. It is a bit larger than the state of California and nearly twice the size of Great Britain. Sweden is 977 miles (1,572 kilometers) long, covers 173,732 square miles (449,964 square kilometers), and is 310 miles (499 kilometers) wide at its widest point.

The country covers the eastern side of the Scandinavian peninsula, sharing a border with Norway on the west. The Baltic Sea forms a natural boundary around the southern tip of Sweden, with the Gulf of Bothnia and Finland providing the eastern and northeastern borders.

Since the country is so long, the weather varies from one end of the "herring" to another. The head (the south) is usually warm and the tail (the north) is often cold. The Swedish climate is affected by the warm waters of the North Atlantic Drift, the

The midnight sun on Midsummer Eve at Lake Torne, north of the Arctic Circle

pleasantly comfortable ocean current that sweeps up the Atlantic. During the winter, northern Sweden is frosty and snowbound between December and March. Elsewhere, the amount of snow varies from region to region.

THE MIDNIGHT SUN

Northern Sweden is called the Land of the Midnight Sun. One seventh of Sweden is north of the Arctic Circle. Here, the sun never sets for several weeks in June and July. It never really gets dark for weeks throughout the summer. This makes it hard to sleep, but the Swedes have devised heavy blinds for their windows to keep out the lengthy daylight.

On the other hand, in the winter, the sun never rises north of the Arctic Circle.

Logging is one of the important industries of Sweden.

More than fifteen thousand years ago, Sweden was crunched and battered by glaciers. These giant heaps of ice moved over the Scandinavian peninsula like bulldozers, pushing mud and rocks in front of them. When the glaciers finally melted, a ridge of mountains remained along the center of Scandinavia. Sweden and Norway share this rocky rib cage along their northern borders. The highest peaks in Sweden are 6,900 feet (2,103 meters) tall. In southern Sweden, the glaciers sheared off the top of the mountains, leaving a high plateau.

Hikers, skiers, mountain climbers, hunters, and fishermen find the north, the Norrland, perfect for sport. This is mostly logging country; logging is one of the principal industries of Sweden. Farming and factories are the mainstays of the flatlands in the south.

A ferry from Denmark nears Helsingborg harbor.

Sweden is only a short distance from the North Sea. The sea can be reached by a narrow channel that separates Sweden from Denmark. It takes little time to cross by ferryboat, so Danes and Swedes are always buzzing back and forth.

There are 4,700 miles (7,564 kilometers) of coastline, beginning at the Norwegian border just below Oslo, swinging to the south and running up to the Finnish border at the Gulf of Bothnia. Unlike Norway, Sweden has few fjords, those deep water inlets stabbing the mountains from the sea. But she does have thousands of tiny islands just offshore. They shelter the mainland and serve as perfect hideaways for city folks on vacation. In very grim winters, when wicked Arctic winds howl out of the north and the

Farmland in southern Sweden

snow is higher than the eaves of a house, the entire coast of Sweden is locked in ice from November to May.

Swedes protect their environment. Even manufacturing plants seem to be a part of the forests. Nothing is out of place with the landscape. There is little grime in the air because much of the electrical power for factories is generated by hydroelectric plants. The might and strength of waterfalls and rivers have been put to good use.

Only about 9 percent of the country is suitable for farming, with the best fields located in the southern "breadbasket." The first settlers fell in love with the rolling meadows. Their ancient stone houses are crumbling now, the ruins of past civilizations.

Gripsholm Castle, on an island on Lake Mälaren, is now a museum. It dates back to the 1300s.

CHATEAUX COUNTRY

Southern Sweden is called "Skane" (pronounced "scone-eh"). Throughout the ages, so many rich people built huge manors and tended vast estates that the province got the nickname of Chateaux Country. There are more than two hundred fortified castles and stately homes dotting the hills. Many have been restored and are open to the public. Some eighteenth-century inns have been converted into restaurants.

The Vikings burst out of Skåne hundreds of years ago, carrying their message of fire and death. Allied with their Norwegian and Danish cousins, the Swedish Vikings were the scourge of the seas

Skåne (right) has beautiful fertile plains. The city of Lund (left) has cobbled streets, medieval buildings, and a university that opened in 1668.

for generations. Not all Vikings were oceangoing warriors, however. Many stayed at home to till the fields, build beautiful ships, and make certain the homeland was safe from enemies.

In medieval times, the cities along the Skåne coast—such as Malmö and Helsingborg—were active trading ports. In the seventeenth century, Denmark controlled this province on and off for years. As a result, the residents have a special dialect different from the rest of Sweden. They also have their own provincial flag and a brand of schnapps (a liqueur) that is very strong.

A TOUGH BREED

The large province to the north of Skåne is Småland. There is a legend explaining why this area is much more harsh and rocky

The land is rugged on the west coast.

than Skåne. Supposedly when the Lord was making Skåne so beautiful and fertile, the Devil sneaked past him and transformed Småland into a desolate, windswept place crowded with stones and woods. By the time the Lord caught up with the Devil, it was too late to make any changes in the landscape.

So the Lord told the Devil, "You made the countryside, but I get to make the people." He did—producing a tough and stubborn breed of Swedes who were able to use their rocky land to the best advantage. It's been said that if someone born in Småland is put on a barren island with only an ax, he'll manage to have a garden growing within a week or so!

Småland is called "Crystal Country" because of the many glassworks located there. Famous manufacturers such as Orrefors,

An artisan blowing glass at the Orrefors glass factory

Kosta, Boda, and Lindshammar are well known throughout the world. There is a very interesting glass museum in the little town of Växjö. Smålanders are noted for all sorts of other crafts as well, especially furniture making. Many of them live in little workshop communities called "bruk."

The next door provinces of Blekinge and Östergötland complete the tier of southern Sweden. Both are great vacation spots for Swedish city dwellers who enjoy biking and hiking. Sweden's Lake Vänern, 90 miles (145 kilometers) long and 50 miles (80 kilometers) wide, is here—the largest lake in all of Europe. It is one link in a 350-mile (563-kilometer) waterway connecting the major cities of Göteborg and Stockholm. The Gota Canal, which

Left: Opening one of the locks on the Gota Canal
Right: Midsummer Eve celebration

opened in 1932 and has sixty-five locks, makes up 115 miles (185 kilometers) of the waterway. The canal is the longest ship channel in the world, but is no longer used much except for pleasure boats. It is not deep enough for today's commerical freighters.

Every province of Sweden has its own customs and distinctive local costumes. In the heart of Sweden are Värmland and Dalarna, called the "Folklore Provinces" by tourist officials. People here are more inclined to dress up for their numerous festivals. On Midsummer Eve, maypoles are raised in every village and everyone turns out to dance. Many of Sweden's greatest writers came from this area.

More than half of Sweden is covered with forests.

There is a great deal of heavy industry in central Sweden, from the Bofors armaments company to the copper mines and smelters around Falun.

LEFT FROM GLACIER DAYS

Flying over northern Sweden is like flying over a green ocean. Everywhere below, from horizon to horizon, are the thick forests. Only 17 percent of Sweden's population lives here, working in the timber mills, the ironworks, or at hydroelectric stations.

Skiers flock to the north to try terrain left from glacier days, ranging from gentle slopes to the sheer ridges of the Helag

Rock paintings from the Bronze Age have been found in Bohuslän province north of Göteborg.

Mountains. The highest road in Sweden, at 3,000 feet (914 meters) above sea level, cuts across the mountains. On some of the cliff sides are rock paintings made centuries ago by Sweden's ancestors.

Lake Storsjön, the Great Lake, is a principal attraction in the province of Jämtland. Prehistoric tribes settled around the lake, offering sacrifices to their gods. The "ting," a clan council for those ancient people, also met there often. Today, pagans are simply the stuff of legends. Tourists have replaced them. Jämtland has hosted a world ski championship on Mount Åre and is the training center for Sweden's Olympic champions in cross-country skiing and running.

The Lapps use red, yellow, and blue in their costumes.

LAND OF THE LAPPS

There is nothing more dramatic in all of Sweden than Lapland, a rocky, wooded region that actually extends all the way from Norway to Finland, crossing Sweden's northernmost point.

The migratory Lapps, of a different racial stock than the Germanic Swedes, live here year round—herding reindeer and cutting timber. The Lapps probably came from Asia, rather than from Europe as did most of the forerunners of the Swedes. The Lapps are shorter and darker than their Teutonic neighbors and speak a different language.

The rivers slice through the woods in an easterly direction from the mountain range along the Norwegian border to the Swedish

Anyone who goes north across these white stones will be in the Arctic.

coast, making it easy to float logs out of the wilderness to the sawmills.

About 60 miles (96 kilometers) north of the town of Boden a line of white stones extends on either side of the railroad track. This marks the Arctic Circle.

There are many iron ore mines throughout Lapland, especially around Gällivare. Scientists estimate that ore reserves there measure about 400,000,000 tons (362,880,015 metric tonnes). Above ground, a chair lift rises to the top of Dundret (Thunder Mountain). At 2,500 feet (762 meters) above sea level, the view of the Midnight Sun is amazing.

Actually the Midnight Sun is not as dark as many photos suggest. They were probably taken with a filter, shooting directly

A railroad station just south of the Arctic Circle

into the sun, giving the appearance of evening. Usually, the light is as bright as ordinary light an hour or so before sunset. It seems very strange, though, to have that much light last all night long.

Riksgränsen is the last Swedish outpost in the north before crossing into Norway. A tiny railroad station there doubles as a customs post. Cross-country skiers scoot across the border here because it is a natural way to enter or leave Sweden. The wide snowfields in the district are perfect for training runs.

Each area of Sweden, from south to north, has its special charms. It is a land of lakes and forests. It is a nation of delightful geographic contrasts, with a new sight around each bend in the road.

Evidence of early settlements have been found in
Sweden. Strange rock formations along the coast in
Gotland (above), runic (Viking) writing (bottom left),
and burial mounds from the fifth century (bottom right)
in Uppsala attest to some early civilizations.

Chapter 3
SWEDEN IN HISTORY

Thousands of years ago, prehistoric men and women wandered over the fertile fields of southern Sweden, following the retreating glaciers and looking for game. They settled, built crude stone homes, and eventually disappeared, leaving behind only a few artifacts from their society—just enough to tantalize archaeologists.

The first known people of Sweden were the Svears, a tribe called the Suiones by the Roman historian Tacitus in the late first century B.C. They were a rough and warlike lot, constantly fighting with their neighbors. The Svears, probably descendants of Germanic tribes who had wandered north across Denmark, hated the folks who already lived in Götaland. They were supposedly the ancestors of the Goths, who returned to Europe because of the ferocity of the Svears. The Goths, or Swedish "Götar," became tired of being picked on. They made their way back south, eventually to take over the tattered remains of the Roman Empire. Those few Götar who remained were eventually absorbed by the Svear tribes.

The Russians called the Swedish Vikings Varangians.

THE SWEDISH VIKING

The merger of these primitive cultures gave rise to the Swedish Viking, a truly formidable man who usually enjoyed raiding more than tending crops. While Danish and Norwegian Vikings were marauding along the European coasts and in Great Britain, the Swedish Vikings turned to the east. They were called the Varangians by the Russians, who had to contend with their attacks for generations in the seventh and eighth centuries.

These tall, blond warriors pillaged and looted all the way through Russia to the Black and Caspian seas, using the rivers as highways for their fleets. One Swede named Rurik founded Novgorod in 862; it became one of the earliest Russian cities of any importance. Some Varangians even made it into Turkey and Arabia, where they became imperial guards for the royal courts.

Rurik founded the Russian city of Novgorod in 862.

No one could match their terrible war axes and battle swords, so they held sway for years. Eventually, however, they intermarried with numerous eastern European people and settled down, adopting the Slavic culture and forgetting their Swedish woods and lakes.

Saint Ansgar attempted to introduce Christianity to the Swedes who stayed at home during the late 800s. The people, however, were mostly pagans with no interest in Ansgar's message. The Swedes were never really totally converted until four hundred years later when all the clans were brought under the wing of Eric IX. It was under Eric's leadership that Finland was conquered by Sweden.

Eric was attending mass when a disgruntled Danish prince stabbed him. His death earned Eric a sainthood and he eventually was made patron of Sweden. His feast day is May 18.

Visby was a shipping center in the Middle Ages.

A TIME OF WAITING

For a long time after Eric and the robust days of the Vikings, Sweden sat back and preferred to watch the world pass by. The country was ruled by petty kings who cared little about bringing in new ideas or trading with neighboring lands.

It was up to individual cities to seek markets for Swedish goods. One of the foremost was Visby on the Baltic island of Gotland, which served as an outpost for the Hanseatic League. The league was a confederation of powerful merchant towns along the rim of northern Europe. In the early Middle Ages, they controlled most of the trade throughout the known world. However, many Swedes didn't mind if outsiders visited their ports. The foreigners would naturally have to pay Swedish taxes, which in those days

Queen Margaret of Denmark formed the Kalmar Union. The Swedes rose up against Eric of Pomerania (being crowned by Margaret) to end the Kalmar Union.

were usually in the form of trade goods. The Swedes thought that was a much better idea than going abroad themselves and having to pay taxes to somebody else.

The only important source of information flowing from the outside world was the Catholic church. Christianity had finally flowered in Sweden and most people were fairly religious. The church was very powerful; eventually it owned more than 20 percent of all Swedish land.

In 1319, Sweden and Norway were united by Magnus VII. In 1397, Queen Margaret added Denmark to the list of territories — the resulting combination of countries being called the Kalmar Union. Eventually, the center of power moved to Denmark, while Sweden was run by regents who represented the Danish crown. They had a difficult time both controlling the peasants and keeping on good terms with the Catholic church.

Vadstena Castle was founded by King Gustaf Vasa in 1545.

The Swedish peasants, though, had more influence in those days than did the lower classes throughout the rest of Europe. They were represented in the Diet assemblies (the parliament) that met every few years to impose taxes, elect the regents, and discuss affairs of state. But the peasants' influence was small compared to the power of the clergy and the merchants. Also, the peasants were taxed on their property, while the nobility and the clergy didn't have to pay taxes.

OF KINGS AND CHURCHES

Christian II, king of Denmark, tried to reassert his control over Sweden and ordered the massacre of many Swedish noble families in 1520. The "Stockholm Bloodbath" subsequently became legendary. This heavy-handed tactic helped lead to a rebellion

Gustaf Vasa was king of Sweden for more than twenty years.

under the leadership of Gustaf Eriksson Vasa, the nephew of a former queen of Sweden.

With the support of the peasants, Gustaf and a handful of German mercenaries drove the Danes from Sweden. In 1523, he was elected king, a position he held for more than twenty years. He had the Diet approve a hereditary monarchy, using his own family as the base of the new succession of power.

Gustaf got into a lengthy argument with the Catholic pope over the appointment of bishops. He settled the argument by confiscating all the church lands, expelling the Catholics, and inviting Lutherans to come to Sweden. Ever since, the Protestant church has been the state church of Sweden.

The country was eventually drawn into troubles on the European continent. To protect her province of Finland, Sweden expanded her navy and soon controlled all of the Baltic Sea. This cut off the Russians from access to the huge inland sea.

Gustavus Adolphus was killed in the Battle of Lutzen.

Furthermore, the Poles and the Germans could use the sea only if the Swedes gave their approval.

OF KINGS AND ARMIES

These policies naturally caused ill feelings and the time grew ripe for war. The House of Hapsburg, a major Catholic power from central Europe, wanted to crush the power of the Protestants—for both religious and financial reasons. Gustavus Adolphus, the grandson of Gustaf Vasa, decided to enter the fray on behalf of the Protestants. Thus began the horrible Thirty Years War that devasted most of Europe in the mid-1600s.

With Dutch allies, the mighty Swedish military machine rolled across Poland and into Germany. The Swedes won almost every battle because of their discipline, bravery, and mobile cannon. But Gustavus Adolphus was killed in the Battle of Lutzen in November, 1632. No other military commander was considered good enough to replace him, so the Swedes retreated.

Charles XII, king from 1697 to 1718

By the time the peace treaty was signed in 1648, Sweden was lucky to keep a few outposts on the southern shores of the Baltic. In the years that followed, Swedish kings often tried to recapture some of their lost territory. Charles XII became king in 1697 when he was only fifteen. He, too, built a mighty army that defeated almost everyone it met. The Swedes were finally beaten while on their way to attack Moscow in 1709. Charles was imprisoned in Turkey until 1715 and was killed trying to capture a Norwegian fort three years later.

After the death of Charles XII, Sweden turned its attention to the domestic scene, taking a break from warfare. The nobles, the peasants, the merchants, and the royalty jockeyed for more power. Political parties were formed, with one faction being called the Hats and another the Caps. The Hats wanted to go to war with Russia; the Caps favored peace.

Drottningholm Theater

During the latter part of the eighteenth century, under King Gustav III, Sweden experienced its cultural Golden Age. The Royal Opera, the Royal Ballet, the Swedish Academy (which eventually would be given the job of choosing the winners of the fabled Nobel Prize in literature), and the Drottningholm Theater were established. Gustav was assassinated, however, by some noblemen. His son, Gustav IV Adolf, succeeded to the throne.

THE LAST WARS

Gustav IV Adolf entered the Napoleonic Wars on the side of England against the French. While the Swedes were fighting elsewhere, the Russians saw an opportunity to capture Finland, which they did in 1809. Thus Sweden was reduced to its current

Jean Baptiste Bernadotte

size. The Swedes blamed Gustav Adolf for this and replaced him. The new king was Charles XIII, but he soon died childless.

An heir to the throne was sought outside the Vasa dynasty founded so many years earlier. Elected was Jean Baptiste Bernadotte, one of Napoleon's field marshals. Bernadotte brought the Swedes back into the European wars, this time against his old friend Napoleon. He was named Charles XIV Johan in 1818 and forced the Danes to give him Norway as a prize after the Napoleonic Wars ended.

So during those troubled times, Finland was lost and Norway was gained as a territory (and held until 1905). But the Napoleonic Wars were the last wars ever fought by Swedish armies. Ever since then, the Swedes have been at peace.

Above: Hay is grown in Gotland, Sweden's largest island.
Below: Gallerian *is a shopping arcade in downtown Stockholm.*

Chapter 4
SWEDEN TO TODAY

Modern Sweden grew up slowly but not without some pain. The peasants wanted to retain their old ways and constantly rejected any change. For generations, they had lived in villages. Every villager had a narrow strip in each of the fields outside of town and could own as many as one hundred of these plots.

A DEMAND FOR CHANGE

The open field system had developed during the Middle Ages to make sure that everyone had a piece of land to farm. However, the plots were too narrow to be cultivated independently. No villager could raise different crops than his neighbor raised. The system was very rigid, but one that the peasants seemed to want. Why? Because it had always, always been done that way.

The demand for change came from the nobles who saw that this type of farming was neither efficient nor profitable. They sent out government surveyors to open up the fields. The farmers were angry because they felt some people got more land than they deserved under the new property laws. Some historians say that this disruption of the fabric of Swedish society was bad.

Instead of helping each other as they had when living in villages, the peasants isolated themselves from the rest of their communities when they built homes on their new, larger plots. Yet, slowly, agricultural production did finally improve. The farmers still didn't trust the upper classes, though, after the breakup of the community land.

The Diet decided in 1842 to introduce compulsory school education. Each parish was required to have a teacher and a school. As children went through the system, they began to seek new friends. Before long, a spirit of independence grew. Many young people dropped out of church, feeling that the state Lutheran church was too close to the ruling class. Trade unions expanded, although they were opposed by the state church, which considered the organizations too liberal.

A TIME TO EMIGRATE

The population expanded from 1,500,000 in 1720 to 2,400,000 in 1810, to about 3,500,000 in 1850. The peasants were unable to keep up with the demands for food, despite the land reforms. Poverty and poor harvests went hand in hand.

Many Swedes decided it was time to emigrate. They left Sweden to look for a better life elsewhere. During the 1880s, at least 325,000 Swedes out of the total population of 4 million went to the United States. Many others went elsewhere.

Over the next twenty years, between 10,000 and 20,000 Swedes moved to America each year, many settling in the Midwest

During World War II, Raoul Wallenberg, a Swedish diplomat, issued Swedish passports to more than twenty thousand Jews giving them citizenship in a neutral country and saving them from extermination by the Nazis. Wallenberg disappeared in 1945.

because the land was similar to that of the Old Country. Today, many Swedes have relatives living in the United States.

During the last 150 years, Sweden has edged its way forward in many fields. Economically, politically, and socially, it has turned toward the future, rather than cling to the past. Industrialization, which started in the late nineteenth century, created radical changes on the face of Sweden. No longer was the country basically rural. More and more people moved to the cities to be close to the factories.

Along with the rise of manufacturing came the rise of the Social Democratic party, which dominated politics after World War I. Throughout this time, the Swedes maintained their political neutrality, even through the bloody days of both world wars. The country became a haven for people fleeing oppressive governments elsewhere during the war years. This neutrality was stretched a bit, however, during the 1940s, when many young Norwegians were trained as "Swedish policemen." They then returned to their homeland as guerrilla fighters against the German Nazis, who had conquered Norway.

After the war, the need for more workers intensified. Many residents of other countries—especially Yugoslavia and Turkey—moved to Sweden to live. A great number of them became citizens.

KEEPING WITH THE TIMES

Through all these changes, Sweden retained its monarchy. The current king is Carl XVI Gustav, who came to the throne in 1973 at twenty-seven years of age. He took as his motto "For Sweden— In Keeping With the Times." King Carl Gustav and his wife, Queen Silvia, have three children: Crown Princess Victoria, who was born on July 14, 1977; Prince Carl Philip, born May 13, 1979; and Princess Madeleine, born June 10, 1982. Under the Act of Succession of 1980, the throne of Sweden will pass to the oldest child of the king and queen, regardless of sex. So Princess Victoria someday will likely be queen of Sweden.

Under the Swedish constitution, which was revised in 1974, the king is head of state. His duties are more ceremonial than official. For instance, he annually opens the beginning session of the Riksdag (which had been called the Diet in the old days), is chairman of the foreign affairs advisory council, receives foreign dignitaries, and represents Sweden in other countries.

The king and queen are very popular. Carl Gustav loves sailing, hunting, and fishing. He has made a reputation for himself in nature conservation, taking part in United Nations conferences on

King Carl XVI and Queen Silvia

the environment and playing an active role in the World Wildlife Fund. He is a great supporter of scouting and is honorary chairman of the World Organization of the Scout Movement.

Queen Silvia is the daughter of a West German businessman who married a Brazilian woman. She is very active in sports and was chief hostess for the organizing committee of the Olympic games in Munich in 1972—where she met the then Crown Prince Carl Gustav. They were married on June 19, 1976, in Storkyrkan, the cathedral in Stockholm.

A RIKSDAG DEMOCRACY

Even with a king, Sweden is still a parliamentary democracy. Every three years, each Swede over eighteen votes for

The Riksdag

representatives to the Riksdag, or parliament. Candidates are put up by political parties, of which there are five major organizations and several smaller ones. In the general elections, 349 men and women are chosen to sit in the Riksdag, which makes the laws.

At the same time the Riksdag members are elected, voting is held for municipal officials. The local councils determine how much money the towns need to operate schools, determine the services for the elderly, and perform similar important jobs.

The party that gets the highest number of votes in an election also gets the most seats in the Riksdag. This party then appoints the ministers, who make up the cabinet—or the government. Each minister is in charge of a governmental department, such as justice, housing, or economic affairs. The government is headed by a prime minister, who is the true leader of Sweden.

A government falls if the Riksdag doesn't support the prime minister and his cabinet. A new government then has to be chosen.

Elections in Sweden are exciting. People take their right to vote very seriously; at least 90 percent of the eligible voters always go to the polls. For a number of years, the Socialist and non-Socialist parties captured almost an equal number of votes. From 1976 to 1982, the non-Socialists were in power—holding just a slight edge over their opponents. The Social Democrats took control after the 1982 parliamentary elections.

Sweden's civil service has traditions that go back to the seventeenth century. While ministers come and go, the civil servants are nonpolitical, professional governmental workers. They make sure Sweden runs smoothly and efficiently.

OMBUDSMEN AND JUSTICE

In the nineteenth century Sweden created a unique department. The Riksdag appointed an official called an ombudsman. This person investigates citizens' complaints about government decisions or actions. A few years later a second ombudsman was appointed to cover the military. Since then, other countries have followed Sweden's example so that citizens' questions and complaints will be heard.

The Swedes keep a close watch over their elected officials and the government in cooperation with the ombudsman. Most agencies are open to the press, which plays an important watchdog role in Swedish society. Journalists can inspect almost any government document or file to make certain no one is cheating, stealing, or abusing power while in office.

Swedish justice is based on written law that has evolved over the years since the Viking days. The court system is organized on three levels, with the highest being the Supreme Court.

There are very few prisons in Sweden that fit the worldwide picture—vast blocks of stone and steel. Swedish prisoners are sent to jail for rehabilitation and usually perform some work there. The slogan of the Correctional Administration is "First we build the factory and then we add the prison." Often, the convicts have to pay room and board if they have a job making good wages.

SOCIAL WELFARE: BENEFITS, NOT GIFTS

Sweden has undergone numerous changes in her social system during the twentieth century. The first national pension plan went into effect in 1913. In 1931, regional and local health insurance programs were introduced. There is now a national compulsory health insurance plan that was started in 1955.

High taxes allow the government to provide liberal benefits for all citizens. Pregnant women can take leaves of absence from their jobs for childbirth. Tax allowances are given for each child under sixteen and each child in secondary school or university.

Employees are legally guaranteed four-week vacations with pay. Unemployment compensation is generous, as are retirement benefits. Pensions are provided for widows, orphans, and children who have lost one parent.

It has always been the idea in Sweden that the allowances and insurance were not gifts to the needy, but benefits to which all citizens were entitled. Benefits became rights guaranteed by law.

All hospital treatment in Sweden is free. Private doctors may charge extra for special services, but the government reimburses

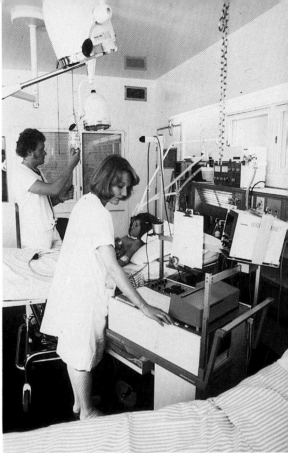

The standard of living is high in Sweden. Most day nurseries and health care facilities are free.

the patient for up to three fourths of the fee. There are numerous other medical benefits as well, in addition to allowances given to mothers at the birth of a child.

Swedes probably have the most extensive network of social benefits of any Western country. Day nurseries help working mothers; old age homes are being built. Swedes are used to their high standard of living. Almost 90 percent of welfare spending goes to people for reasons of age, family conditions, or health, not for reasons of lack of income.

As one writer said, "The more the Swedes have, the more they have to lose and the welfare state has been fashioned to make sure there are no losers."

Danderyd Hospital in a suburb of Stockholm

WEALTH, HEALTH, AND HOUSING

Sweden's wealth is therefore broadly shared by all the population. A low child mortality rate and a high average age are two indications of secure living conditions. Today, most Swedes are skilled industrial or office workers. There is little difference between the two groups. Their living standards are the same. They usually make similar amounts of money. They live next door to each other.

The so-called poor in Sweden are those who don't have a full-time income, probably due to a physical or mental handicap. The welfare system in Sweden hopes to narrow the gap between the haves and these have-nots.

Of course, the demands for services have put a strain on the Swedes. Often, there are long waits for nonemergency medical care. In fact, there was one plan to open a hospital in Italy, where the overflow of Swedish patients could go to be treated by Italian

Swedish designers are known throughout the world for their functional kitchens.

doctors. The Swedish government was to foot the bill for its citizens who went there.

Housing shortages are still common, especially in the large cities. For a while, towering apartments were being constructed—not really the best places to raise children. Now more and more people are eagerly looking for individual houses. Many people have a second home in the forest where they spend their vacations.

Swedish design in housing, especially in functional areas such as kitchens, is world renowned for its layout and efficiency. Everything seems to be neat and trim and in its place.

THE EQUALITY OF WOMEN

Women are guaranteed equal rights in Sweden. Governmental officials and committees keep close watch to make sure that women are treated fairly in the work force and at home. Of

Left to right: Greta Garbo, Ingrid Bergman (movie actresses), and Jenny Lind (soprano)

Sweden's eight million citizens, more than half are female. About 75 percent of the women work outside the home, with approximately 58 percent of that number being married. Of the married women aged sixteen to sixty-four who are working, 42 percent have children under sixteen. Most families have only one or two children.

An Act of Equality, passed in 1980, aims to officially promote equal rights for women. Fines can be imposed on companies taking advantage of their female work force. But women at home often end up doing most of the housework and looking after the children.

This is a factor attacked by many women's movement leaders in Sweden, such as Eva Moberg and Kristina Ahlmark-Michanek. Both have written numerous articles and books about the role of women in Swedish society and the importance of freeing women to make use of their talents and intelligence.

Women in Sweden play a much more active role in public life

Left: Women's rights champion Fredrika Bremer. Right: Alva and Gunnar Myrdal

than in many other countries. At least ninety-two members of the Riksdag are female. Five of eighteen members of a recent cabinet of ministers were women. The average is the same on local and regional governmental levels as well. A century ago, Fredrika Bremer was a champion for women's rights in Sweden, as was Ellen Key. Singer Jenny Lind (a nineteenth-century performer nicknamed "The Swedish Nightingale"), movie actresses Greta Garbo and Ingrid Bergman, and hundreds of others have been notable world figures.

One of the cowinners of the 1982 Nobel Peace Prize was Swedish sociologist Alva Myrdal, who worked for years trying to advance the cause of military disarmament. She had been a cabinet minister in Sweden from 1967 to 1973. (Her husband, Gunnar, won the Nobel Prize in economics in 1974.)

This bubbling of ideas, this quest for equality, this drive to help each member of Swedish society makes the country an exciting place in which to live.

Stockholm's islands are connected by over forty bridges.

Chapter 5

SWEDEN'S DELIGHTFUL CITIES

Many visitors to Stockholm call the Swedish capital the most beautiful city in the world. Light bathes the church spires, the parks, and the lagoons in an unreal way at dawn every day. It is a city made for discovery.

Stockholm's many parks, squares, and boulevards bring the woodsy feel of Sweden home to its people. It is hard to believe that a century ago only 100,000 people resided in Stockholm. Today, the population has grown to more than a million.

A CAPITAL BEGINNING

A Viking saga explains the origins of the city. Agne, a warrior from the Ynglinga dynasty, had returned from plundering treasure in Finland. As part of the booty, he had captured a chieftain's daughter named Skjalf. On his way home, Agne stopped on the shore of an island that is now part of Stockholm. There he gave a party in honor of his new—if unwilling—bride. The Swedes drank too much mead, that heady beerlike alcohol, and fell asleep. Brave Skjalf freed some fellow Finns who had also been captured; together they hanged Agne and his warriors and returned safely home. The place was subsequently called Agnefit, or Agne Strand.

Stockholm dropped from sight until 1252, when preserved chronicles indicate that a powerful king named Birger Jarl founded a fortified castle on the location of the present city. From those beginnings, Swedes mark off the growth of their capital in four stages: those early years; the arrival of King Gustav Vasa, who made Stockholm a capital in 1523; the heart of Gustavus Adolphus's empire a century later; and modern times.

Gustav Vasa, known as the Father of Sweden, kept his jewels and money in the Stockholm Royal Palace while he moved about the country to keep an eye on things. Subsequent kings stayed closer to home—they didn't want to lose sight of the royal treasure. Later, Gustavus Adolphus needed a place to train his troops and a base for his administration. Just before he left on the military campaign in which he was killed, Gustavus told the citizens of Stockholm that he hoped that everyone eventually would live in large stone houses.

As the years went by, just about everybody did get a stone house. Even though wars were devastating Europe, Sweden was never invaded. Stockholm could grow peacefully, dozing in the sun. As late as 1860, Stockholm's main street still had no sidewalks. But in that same year, the first train in Sweden chugged into town from Södertälje, only twenty-five miles (forty kilometers) away. It brought a new age to the sleepy capital.

Boats are one means of transportation in Stockholm.

STOCKHOLM TODAY

Over the last hundred years, Stockholm finally has reached maturity. The city spread over twelve islands before settling down on the mainland. In fact, Stockholm resembles Italy's Venice because of all the waterways between its neighborhoods. Two sprawling suburbs spread out on either side: Vällingby on the west and Farsta on the south are connected by a modern subway system called the T-bana.

Although Stockholm is large, it is easy to get around in. The islands and their forty-two connecting bridges break up the city into sections. The Old Town is in the center, with its adjoining islands called Riddarholmen (Knights' Island) and Helgeandsholmen (Island of the Holy Spirit). Norrmalm is the financial and commercial section; most of the offices of the city government are on Kungsholmen. Many embassies and consulates

The Stockholm Royal Palace was rebuilt after the fire in 1697.

are on the residential island of Östermalm. Djurgården is mostly parkland, with museums, an amusement park, and many restaurants.

The sprawling Stockholm Royal Palace is noted for its openness. Anyone can walk in and out of the gates freely. The original palace was the Three Crowns. It was destroyed by fire in 1697, but was immediately rebuilt. Directly across from the palace is the Great Church, the Stockholm cathedral and the oldest building in the city, dating from 1250.

One old street near the palace is the narrowest roadway in the world still used and maintained by a city. It is called Mårten Trotzigs Gränd (Yard-wide Lane).

The Swedes are proud of the restoration work they have done on the *Vasa*, a seventeenth-century man-of-war that sank the same day it was launched in 1628. Naturally, everyone was, and is, a bit embarrassed that the ship never made it out of the harbor

Left: Marten Trotzigs Gränd (Yard-wide Lane) in the Old Town
Right: The warship Vasa *from the seventeenth century is in the Vasa Museum.*

on her maiden voyage. The Swedes are known for building things that work. They finally raised the vessel in 1961, refurbished it as it was when new, and placed it in a museum.

Stockholm is noted for its fine museums: the National Museum of Fine Arts, the Museum of Modern Arts, the National Museum of Antiquities and Royal Cabinet of Coins, the Nordic Museum, Thiel Art Gallery, the Swedish Museum of Natural History, the Museum of Music, the National Maritime Museum, the Technical Museum, the Royal Armory, and Skansen, an open-air museum on a hill overlooking the city. There are dozens more: The Swedes like to remain in touch with their past, as well as showcase their artists of today.

From Stockholm, located almost in the midsection of this long, narrow country, the visitor can travel anywhere and find cities and towns equally as charming as the capital.

Above: Riddarholm Church, on the tiny island of Riddarholmen next to the Old Town, is the burial place of Swedish kings and queens.
Left: A child admires a sculptured swan in one of Stockholm's parks.

Left: A farmers' market in a modern section of Stockholm. Above: Kungsträdgården (Kings Garden), a large park in downtown Stockholm. Below: The National Maritime Museum traces the history of the Swedish navy and merchant marine.

SAINTS AND SKERRIES

The Valley of Lake Mälaren, just inland from Stockholm, has been settled since Viking days. Birka, one of Sweden's ancient capitals, was once a major trade center on the long route between Russia and western Europe. Not much is left of Birka except for remains of old forts and some burial mounds. Legends indicate this was the first place Saint Ansgar preached to the pagan Swedes. There is a large cross in Birka erected to his memory — and to his patience. It took generations to convert the stubborn Swedes to Christianity.

Scattered around Stockholm are thousands of tiny islands called Skärgården, or Garden of Skerries. (A skerry is a rocky island.) Many vacation homes dot these little hunks of rock and trees. But there are also some top-secret military bases located in parts of this Stockholm archipelago. In the 1980s, submarines from Eastern bloc nations tried to sneak in for a closer look at the facilities. The Swedes, although neutral, have a powerful military force and they chased the subs away.

Things are usually quieter all around Sweden. She has been called "the Neutral Porcupine" because Sweden keeps her nose out of other people's business, yet is ready to defend herself.

A PAGAN BEGINNING

Uppsala is another major Swedish city, almost fifteen hundred years old. Pagans, Christians, politicians, and students have long caroused through its streets. The last pagans disappeared around A.D. 500 at the time of the burial of kings from the Ynglinga dynasty.

Students in white caps celebrate Walpurgis Night.

Christians eventually built a church on the site of a pagan temple. In keeping with its God-fearing tradition, Uppsala is now the residence of the Swedish archbishop, head of the Swedish Lutheran church. On the secular side, over subsequent centuries some Swedish kings made Uppsala their home. The University of Uppsala was founded in 1477, making it the oldest college in northern Europe.

Sometimes, when students cavort on Walpurgis Night (April 30), some of the more staid residents of Uppsala think the pagans are back. That festival dates from heathen days, when people danced around huge bonfires to scare off nighttime demons. It is now the national welcome to spring, with students parading

Liseberg Amusement Park (left) and the harbor at Göteborg (right)

through town in a torchlight procession to the heights near Uppsala Castle. Festivities then continue in student dorms.

A CITY IN THE CENTER

Göteborg, Sweden's second largest city, is sometimes called the "Gateway to the North." It is a hub of shipping, with vessels crowding its large harbor during the freight season. If a triangle is drawn from Stockholm, the Swedish capital, to Copenhagen, the Danish capital, and Oslo, the Norwegian capital, Göteborg is almost dead center in the triangle. Gustavus Adolphus gave the city a charter in 1621 and called in his Dutch allies to help start a shipbuilding industry here.

Göteborg's harbor has 14 miles (22 kilometers) of quays, places

64

for vessels to berth. Two hundred massive cranes lift cargo on and off oceangoing freighters. More than four million tons (3,628,800 metric tonnes) of shipping goes through the port each year, destined for cities all over the world.

Liseberg Amusement Park in Göteborg is one of the best in Europe. There are many beautiful gardens spaced between the carnival rides, restaurants, and concert halls. Like many amusement parks in Scandinavia, its variety shows and open-air musical programs are really top-notch.

SMALL TOWNS AND LARGE

Many smaller Swedish communities might not be well known outside their own country, yet each has a personality shaped either by its citizens, its history, or its environment. The little town of Filipstad, in the Swedish lake district, is one such place. It was the birthplace of John Ericsson, whose ironclad ship *Monitor* defeated the Confederate ironclad *Merrimac* in the American Civil War.

Ericsson, a brilliant engineer, was one of the many thousands of people who emigrated from Sweden during the terrible years of poverty in the 1850s and 1860s. His iron warship secured victory for the Union forces and ushered in a new age. No longer would wooden vessels rule the seas. After he died, the United States returned Ericsson's body to Filipstad where it was buried. His tomb there can still be seen.

The best-known Lapp town in Sweden is Jokkmokk, in the far north. It is a little place, with only about three thousand people—many of whom belong to that nomadic race of people who live in Scandinavia. There is even a Lapp college in town.

Many Lapps live in or near Kiruna. A young boy (left) leans against the door of his family's turf hut and a man poses with his child (right) in front of his tent.

Kiruna is a city where everybody talks about big things. They have every right to brag—because Kiruna is the world's largest town! A few years ago, the whole province was made into a municipality, covering some 8,700 square miles (22,534 square kilometers) of land. It is located at the edge of the tundra north of the Arctic Circle, just where the tree line ends. The center of "town" is a mining area around Kirunavaara, the Iron Mountain. Probably three billion tons (over 2,500,000,000 metric tonnes) of iron ore rest beneath the surface of this giant peak. Kiruna has one of the largest concentrations of such quality ore anyplace in the world.

Kiruna is so large that people tell jokes about its size. Once a man was trying to call a friend on the telephone. He was very hard to reach because he was "out on the town tending his reindeer herd," laugh the Kiruna residents.

Iron ore is mined in Kiruna.

Sweden's highest mountain, Kebnekaise, 6,926 feet (2,111 meters), is also located within the city limits. "It's almost to heaven," assert the residents.

A SKI RACE FOR A KING

Sports fans know all about the little towns of Mora and Sälen, in Dalarna province. Every year, on the first Sunday in March, international cross-country skiers race from Sälen to Mora. More than eight thousand competitors participate in the 55-mile (88-kilometer) contest; tens of thousands of spectators watch, crowding the two towns on race day.

Gustav Vasa supposedly asked the people of Dalarna to join with him in the war against the Danes early in the sixteenth

Medieval wall surrounding Visby

century. At first, the folks refused because they were tired of years of fighting. After they turned him down, Gustaf Vasa decided to leave Sweden and seek refuge in Norway. The peasants changed their minds and sent their fastest skiers racing after their future king. They caught up with him in Sälen. "We'll fight with you," they said. So Gustav Vasa stayed in Sweden, eventually defeating the Danes and changing the course of his country's history.

VISBY AND KALMAR

Visby gives a feeling of life in the Middle Ages. This tidy Swedish town is on the island of Gotland in the Baltic Sea. The city was an outpost of medieval merchants from northern Europe. Surrounding the town is a high wall, left from those days.

Kalmar Castle was used as a fortress to protect the city.

Everywhere are centuries-old buildings, especially churches (at least one hundred on the island).

Visby is also noted for the civic production of *Petrus de Dacia,* a beautiful opera performed each year in the ruins of St. Nicholas Church. Everyone in town turns out to help. In addition, the city is sometimes called "The Town of Roses and Ruins." The ruins are self-evident—they're everywhere. The roses bloom all over the place.

Like many Swedish towns, Kalmar also has a nickname. It is often called "The Lock and Key of Sweden." Whoever controlled Kalmar controlled the coast north to Stockholm. Kalmar was the site of a conference in 1397 that set up the Kalmar Union, an attempt to put all of Scandinavia under one ruler. The castle has a dungeon below the surface of the sea.

Paper and paper products (above) and electrical equipment
(below) are important products manufactured in Sweden.

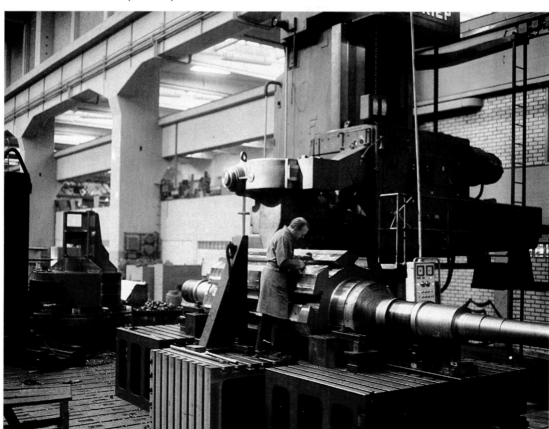

Chapter 6

SWEDEN'S WORKING WORLD

Autos to paper products. Ships to fine crystal. Robots to kitchen matches. Swedish industry produces all sorts of items. The Swedes are noted for their craftsmanship, their technological skill, and the high quality of their finished goods.

The small size of their home market has made many firms international in their outlook. In fact, some companies have more personnel based in other countries than at home. Ninety percent of Swedish industry is privately owned. The rest is owned by the state or by cooperatives. The railways, postal system, communication network, and most of the energy production facilities are also operated by the state.

The cooperatives are very important in Sweden. A co-op is an organization of individuals or companies who get together to make their own goods or sell items to members. The Swedish Cooperative Union and Wholesale Society is one of Sweden's biggest companies. Housing organizations, oil retailers, and insurance firms have also banded together in their own groups. Farmers' groups, too, have formed co-ops, with the Federation of Swedish Farmers being the largest.

JOBS AND UNIONS

Laws regulate private companies. For instance, employees can't be fired without good cause. Other laws allow workers to have a strong voice in decisions made by their companies. The government helps business operations, too. The state lends them money and gives incentives to locate in certain areas, such as the north. Swedish corporate taxes are low, favoring firms that use their profits for investment. Companies that set aside some of their profits in boom years, later using the money for investments during slow years, also get tax breaks.

Many Swedish workers belong to labor unions. At the national level, they are represented by the Swedish Trade Union Confederation (LO in Swedish), which negotiates with the Employers' Confederation (SAF). LO has more than two million members.

White-collar workers, who are not in farming or industry, also have their own unions: the Central Organization of Salaried Employees (TCO) and the Swedish Confederation of Professional Associations (SACO/SR). The LO unions have traditionally been linked with the Social Democratic party, while the other labor groups are independent.

There have been few major labor disputes in Sweden since the 1920s. Since 1928, a National Labor Court has had final approval powers on legal disputes between labor and management.

The court actions have been very helpful in keeping both sides happy. Through union help, the workers now have a forty-hour or less work week. Parents can work six hours a day if they wish, so they can spend more time with their young children. In these cases, they earn less money. All employees also get a minimum of

Many Swedes like to escape to their summer vacation homes to swim and relax.

four paid weeks of vacation every year. July is the most popular holiday month. Almost everything shuts down for that summer escape!

The national government operates an employment service, assisting people in finding jobs or being retrained for new fields. Full employment has always been a priority of all the political parties, regardless of which one is in power. The trade unions offer unemployment insurance for those who are out of work. Those who don't qualify can receive cash grants from the government, which also helps them find other jobs.

ORES AND EXPORTS

Sweden is very dependent on foreign trade. Traditionally, the country has been a supplier of raw materials, such as iron ore. In fact, the Swedish Ironmasters' Association was founded in 1747.

The quality of steel produced from iron ore is excellent.

But now, Sweden is experiencing competition from such countries as Brazil and Australia, which are also exporting ore. Yet the country's reputation for excellent steel still stands, although steel making is only about 7 percent of industrial production. In the nineteenth century, there were some six hundred blast furnaces and forges; today there are about thirty.

A reputation for mining quality ore and producing quality material has helped Sweden remain neutral, both in politics and trade. It was a close call during World War II, however, when the Germans cast their sights on the Swedish mines. They were put off only by threats that the Swedes would blow up the mines, the equipment, and the power sources.

Most Swedish exports go to other European countries. Sweden also is a leader in trade with developing countries in Asia, Latin

Farms in the southwest

and South America, and Africa. The next largest market is with the United States and Canada, followed by eastern Europe.

Sweden has to import much of its fuels, such as oil and gas. It grows most of its own food, except for items like coffee and citrus fruits.

Swedish businesses are changing rapidly, due to mechanization and competition from abroad. Fewer people work in agriculture and logging, but improved techniques have increased production. Fishing is now only a minor industry. Most of the active fishermen work out of the fifty or so harbors around Göteborg on the west coast.

Swedish scientists are continually coming up with new uses for old products. They have been leaders in developing better means of making paper and using wood by-products. But the old ways are just as important in some industries, such as glassmaking.

Beautiful glass products from the Orrefors glass factory

THINGS OF BEAUTY

Orrefors is the best known of the Swedish glass companies. Its dazzlingly beautiful products, and those of the other glassworks, are shipped to the fanciest stores in the world. Traditionally, the best pieces are made in the morning. Smart bargain hunters visiting the district of Kalmar—where most of the firms are located—can get first choice on items of first quality if they show up early enough at the companies' stores.

The basic procedure of glassmaking probably hasn't changed in two thousand years. The red-hot glass is passed back and forth and is twirled and shaped in the process. Scissors are used to cut the glass, which looks like fiery taffy. The finished pieces can be engraved after they have cooled.

Assembly line at a Volvo automobile factory

CARS AND SHIPS AND CHEMICALS

Since the 1950s, Sweden has been the most motorized country in Europe. One out of three Swedes has at least one car—for a total of around 2.9 million passenger cars. There are 190,000 trucks and buses on the roads, as well. Because they appreciate fine autos, the Swedes make fine autos. The Volvo and the Saab/Scania are among the most popular models in the world.

Each firm makes almost 300,000 vehicles a year, plus hundreds of other products ranging from motors to electrical parts. The Swedes cater to the quality conscious buyer, somebody who likes cars as much as they do. That's why there are relatively few Swedish autos made; the workers spend more time on each vehicle. They are highly paid as

A tanker in Göteborg shipyard

a result and have a great deal to say about production.
The use of robots in the auto industry is becoming more
commonplace; however, the final assembly is still done by
skilled humans.

The Swedes also make tankers and commercial freighters for the
world shipping market, as well as oil drilling rigs and other items
used by oceangoing industries. This shipbuilding tradition reaches
back to the days of the early Vasa dynasty.

The country still has a fine merchant fleet of its own, consisting
of three hundred oceangoing vessels and two hundred ships that
dash up and down the coast. Forty-five ferry lines connect the
European mainland with Sweden. Many tankers and freighters
ply the Baltic Sea between northern Europe and Sweden, bringing
in goods and taking out exports. Shipping remains a very
important and profitable business in Sweden.

Left to right: Carl Scheele, Jacob Berzelius, and Alfred Nobel

Chemical products, such as fertilizer, have been made here for more than one hundred years. But it was not until after World War II that chemicals took a strong place in the economy. After the war, chemicals outraced all other industries in growth. In the 1960s, the petrochemical business—utilitizing oil—became very important. Sweden makes ammonia, nitric acid, carbon black, sodium chlorate, and other items that are the basis for different products.

Technical research is highly valued in the chemical industry. Early developments in the field were the results of work by such famous Swedish scientists as Carl Scheele (1742-1786), who discovered oxygen and many other elements; Jacob Berzelius (1779-1848), who introduced the present form of writing chemical

Industry does not destroy the scenery of Gotland.

symbols and formulas; and Alfred Nobel (1833-1896), who invented dynamite. Alfred Nobel left over nine million dollars in his will to establish the Nobel Prizes, which were first awarded in 1901. The Swedes brag proudly that their chemists have discovered more elements than have chemists in any other country, and they are probably correct.

The country is very concerned about maintaining environmental quality. Industry helps keep the landscape clean and fresh. Recycled oil and oil spill residues are used in making ammonia; waste from slaughterhouses and food industries is used for animal feed. Some problems remain, of course, but on the whole, Swedes are confident they can retain the best of their natural surroundings while harvesting the bounty of the land.

Firewood stacked on the island of Gotland. More than half of Sweden is covered with forests.

A KINGDOM OF FORESTS

Sweden's forest industry remains a staple of its economy. Norway pine, Scots pine, birch, and oak make up the bulk of tree varieties. The cool climate is especially good for growing pine. It takes from 70 to 140 years from the time of planting for trees to mature and be ready for harvesting. Because of the cold in northern Sweden, the trees grow slower than in warmer climates.

Most of the public forestlands are in the north, while company forests are in the central part of Sweden and private holdings are in the south.

From the forests the Swedes make board lumber, as well as pulp that can be used in many products. The Swedish Forestry Administration under the direction of the Ministry of Agriculture is responsible for overseeing the timber industry. The forestry workers help woodlot owners plan their harvests, forecast trends,

Logs arrive at a processing center by land and water.

and draw up statistics that help researchers. Under the Ministry of Interior is the Swedish Forest Service, which keeps close track of environmental protection in the forests and around sawmills and pulp factories.

Every March in Stockholm there is a Forest Week that promotes the industry. It features conferences, exhibitions, and displays dealing with lumbering, tree growth, and harvesting techniques.

The Swedish University of Agricultural Sciences offers forestry studies. Many high schools also have one- and two-year courses for machine operators, forest farmers, and plant foremen who work in the woods. The Swedish College of Forestry and its fifteen research departments carefully study everything there is to know about trees, from biology to economic impact. There is even a National Sawmilling School where workers are trained for milling and a National Paper School for workers in the paper industry.

Electric train

The Swedes want to make sure they can protect and nurture this basic industry. They want to keep their Kingdom of the Forests.

HIGHWAYS AND AIRWAYS

Sweden has an extensive network of highways to service its people. Most are located in the south where the bulk of the population lives. But a map outlining traffic volume on the roads shows that even some highways in the far north are used a great deal. These are in the mining and lumbering areas of the Norrland.

As for railroad transportation, Sweden has the most extensive network of railways of any European country—on a per capita basis.

Scandinavian Airlines

Linjeflyg, Sweden's major domestic airline, serves cities all over the country. The international carrier, Scandinavian Airlines (SAS), flies around the world in modern jets. That firm is jointly owned by Danish, Norwegian, and Swedish companies. Each of those in turn is half-owned by their respective governments and half by private individuals. The three countries are proud of their close relationship in air travel.

A MASS OF MEDIA

A long period of peace and economic stability has aided development of the Swedish mass media. The Swedes buy more newspapers and magazines per person than any other people. Almost every household has a radio and most have television sets.

Sweden's freedom of the press has been guaranteed since 1766, by one of the first laws of its kind anywhere.

The 150 newspapers printed in Sweden have a total circulation of 4.8 million. Only seventeen have circulations of more than 50,000; only four have more than 200,000. Almost half of Sweden's newspapers appear three times or less during the week. Much of the Swedish press is allied with some political party, but the government helps by giving production grants and other assistance to papers in trouble or to those who join together for distribution.

There are probably about three thousand periodicals published regularly in Sweden. Religious, political, and temperance groups (those against the drinking of alcohol) publish many magazines, as do trade unions, professional associations, and cultural groups. The average Swede reads at least three magazines a week, in addition to a hometown paper and probably a national circulation paper.

The Swedish Broadcasting Company holds a monopoly on broadcasting, with an annual budget for both radio and television approved by the Riksdag. Neither medium carries any advertising at all. There are three radio channels and two nationwide television networks. Since 1979, neighborhood radio programs run by volunteers have been allowed. These give the ordinary citizen a chance to develop skills in broadcasting and to present more localized versions of events.

Sweden is proud of its industrial base, its cooperation between union and company, and its freedoms. The country works hard to maintain its quality of life, which is one of the highest standards of living in the world today. The Swedish worker helps promote this.

Swedish craftspeople are valued for their skill and efficiency. Above: A student at the Swedish School of Arts, Crafts and Design in Stockholm works on a textile design. Left: An artist paints woodcarved Dala horses.

Chapter 7

TIDE OF CREATIVITY

The arts are important in Swedish life. Swedes love good theater, films, literature, painting, sculpture, and music. They take for granted government support of the arts. Society has a responsibility to provide for a nation's cultural life, they say.

A NATIONAL POLICY

In 1974, the Swedish Riksdag adopted eight goals for its national cultural policy. There was not one vote against the proposals! The eight objectives of the new policy were: to help protect freedom of speech and create conditions necessary for this freedom to be used; to offer people opportunities for creative activity of their own and promote contacts between people; to combat negative effects of "commercialism" in the arts (this means the community should help unemployed artists and promote artistic activity that might not make a lot of money); to spread cultural activities throughout the country; to provide cultural experiences for children, the handicapped, immigrants, minorities, and people living in sparsely populated areas.

The list goes on: to make possible artistic and cultural experiments; to guarantee that the cultural heritage of earlier ages is preserved; and to promote an exchange of experience and ideas with other nations.

Sweden hopes that its people study these ideals and follow them. They are not laws, however, but worthwhile suggestions and guidelines. The Swedish National Council for Cultural Affairs oversees government contributions to theater, dance, music, literature, public libraries, cultural magazines, visual arts, museums, and exhibitions.

The council coordinates governmental subsidies, the money paid to various cultural institutions and organizations to help them operate. It also distributes information on cultural events in Sweden. It helps in research and development of new cultural and artistic activities. The council is therefore very busy.

In drawing up its policy, the Swedish Riksdag went on record that it felt cultural equality—where everyone has access to the arts—is as important as economic and social equality. Everyone should have the chance to develop his or her talents.

Under the national council are county councils, which are responsible for regional activities. There are also ten educational associations that help organize private, amateur artistic activities in Sweden.

PERFORMERS, YEAR-ROUND

The working conditions of Swedish performers are often better than in other countries. For instance, unemployment among

The Royal Dramatic Theater in Stockholm

actors is barely 1 percent in the winter and 4 percent in the
summer. (In the United States unemployment among actors at any
given time might be as high as 90 percent.) Swedish performers
are hired by the year, which means they receive a salary whether
or not they perform. They are also entitled to five to eight weeks
of summer vacation and receive pension and insurance assistance
from their employers. However, many Swedish performers don't
make the amazingly high amounts of money that their
counterparts do in some other nations.

Of course, this does not mean that every artistic activity in
Sweden is a success. For a while, the Swedish film industry was
hurt by the rise in television popularity and by an entertainment
tax on tickets. Book readership declined a bit. It is still sometimes
difficult to convince businesses to support the arts, rather than
letting them depend on the government.

The family, and especially children, is important in Sweden.

This emphasis on the arts and culture is not only aimed at adults but at young people as well. In 1978, the government issued a special report supporting arts and cultural activities for young people. This was called the *Barnen och Kulturen* ("Children and Culture").

READING FOR CHILDREN

Libraries and books form a major link in the chain of Swedish cultural experiences. There are over two thousand libraries scattered throughout the country; each of Sweden's 277 towns has at least one library. It is a law that every school has to have a library. There are also 120 book buses that travel into remote parts of the country. It is an exciting occasion in the Norrland when the book bus arrives!

Sweden had children's libraries as early as 1800, but service was really extended when Valfrid Palmgren-Petersen created a special library in Stockholm in 1911. Similar libraries for children opened about the same time in Malmö and Göteborg.

In addition to providing books, the libraries have storytelling programs, puppet theaters, concerts, meetings with authors, and many other activities. Authors are highly respected in Sweden and young people consider it a great honor to speak with them. In fact, to give writers economic security, they receive a certain amount of money every time one of their books is borrowed from a library.

Children's books have been published in Sweden for years. One of the first was an edition of Aesop's *Fables* in 1603. A magazine for young people was started in 1785. Lewis Carroll's famous *Alice in Wonderland* was translated into Swedish in 1870. Folktales assembled by Gunnar Olof Hyltén-Cavallius in the mid-1800s are still in print today. There are many authors in Sweden who now specialize in young people's literature.

One of the better-known writers is Gunnel Beckman, who often writes about young girls growing up. Inger Brattström is a skilled observer of the world of children, especially when writing about everyday happenings. Rose Lagercrantz, who works as an instructor in children's theater in Stockholm, has written about young people's friendships. Astrid Lindgren wrote the internationally famous books about Pippi Longstocking, a wild and delightful little girl who has exciting and wonderful adventures. Other fine writers' works have been translated and sold throughout the world. In addition, many books from Europe, the United States, and other countries are translated into Swedish.

Sometimes, illustrators for children's books are just as famous as the authors. For instance, Ingrid Vang Nyman, Stig Lindberg, Eva Billow, Ulf Löfgren, and many more are noted for their detailed drawings.

THEATRICAL EXPERIENCES

For any Swede who loves to attend the theater, there are plenty of opportunities to see great drama, dance, and similar programming on the stage. There is a long tradition of theater in Sweden, with such noted playwrights as August Strindberg (1849-1912) and his realistic dramas at the top of the most-famous list.

The major national theatrical companies are the Royal Opera, the Royal Dramatic Theater, and the National Touring Theater. Two world-famous Swedish opera stars of the twentieth century were tenor Jussi Björling and soprano Birgit Nilsson. There are many regional and city theatrical companies that often stage children's plays.

Swedish children are familiar with the "Visiting Theater," which gives performances on playgrounds, in nursery schools—almost anywhere kids gather. One of the first of these little companies was the *Fickteatern* ("The Pocket Theater"), which usually consisted only of three or four actors.

Under the writing of Göran Palm, Siv Widerberg, and Sven Wernström, children saw very controversial plays instead of traditional fairy tales. *The Cream Wolf* told about countries that set up colonies in other lands. Another well-known production was titled *A Play About School.* It concerned the difficulties children can have. The writers wanted children to look at the world around them and ask questions.

Not all young people's theaters travel around the nation. Some are permanently located in cities. Göteborg's Municipal Theater is well known for staging exciting programs for children.

The company once produced a play called *Ostindiefarare* ("The East India Voyager") in which the entire auditorium was

August Strindberg, playwright (left), and Jussi Björling, tenor (right)

converted into a ship. There was even a storm and an attack by pirates. The show, which dealt with a voyage of a Swedish sailor to China in the 1790s, was more than fun and excitement. It told about the hard conditions of the crew on a ship whose owners put profit before safety.

Not long ago, the Stockholm Municipal Theater put on a great play called *Den Svettiga Tigern* (*The Sweaty Tiger*) which was a satire about a cabaret for teenagers.

RADIO, TV, AND FILMS

Radio programs for children started as early as 1925. At first, performers read from books. But eventually, plays were produced for young people. Sometimes, the plays were then made into books—a complete reversal.

As in other countries, television is very popular in Sweden. About half the children's programs viewed in the country are

*Film director
Ingmar Bergman*

purchased from other nations and translated into Swedish. Programs for youngsters are broadcast every day, usually in the late afternoon when they come home from school. There are even special shows for immigrant children and those who have hearing problems.

There have not been many children's movies made in Sweden, although that nation's adult films have been among the world's best—with such actors as Max Von Sydow and directors like Ingmar Bergman.

Producer Arne Suckdorff doesn't believe all movies must have happy endings. Some of his films hit very hard, involving young people in conflicts with grown-ups. Kaj Pollack agrees; he adapts books to the screen, including a publication by Maria Gripe entitled *Elvis, Elvis.*

The Swedish Film Institute operates a children's film department that distributes movies to libraries, schools, and other

Folk, classical, and popular music are enjoyed by the Swedes.

members of Sweden's United Film Studios for Children and Young Adults. The department hopes to provide an alternative to films distributed by the major international companies such as the Walt Disney Studios. After the children watch movies, they are encouraged to discuss what they have seen.

Swedish young people love listening to popular music from the United States, Great Britain, and elsewhere. They buy thousands of records featuring the latest stars. Dance halls and discos are popular. But during the past two decades, more and more young people have begun listening to folk music. And on the classical scene, the National Institute for Concerts organizes musical activities throughout the country, assisted by regional music organizations. Groups travel extensively throughout Sweden to present live performances, many of which are geared toward young people.

Other musical activities are popular. For example, there are at least 250,000 active choral singers in Sweden.

A display of sculpture by Carl Milles

VISUAL AND PUBLIC ARTS

In the visual arts, the Swedes are noted for design and form. Many of their art objects are functional, meaning they can be useful as well as providing visual enjoyment.

Individual craftspeople enjoy a great deal of status in Sweden. Carl Milles is a very famous sculptor. Jeweler Sigurd Persson has been asked to make items ranging from church decorations to silverware for Scandinavian Airlines.

In new residential areas, emphasis is put on access to shops and services. But Swedes consider it important to place art works in public places, as well. Sculptor Roland Haeberlein's works are among the many pieces designed by Swedes to brighten parks, hospitals, fountain areas, boulevards, office centers, and apartment complexes.

*Swedish designers make furniture that
is beautiful as well as functional.*

The Swedes are noted for their fine furniture, textiles and, of course, glass. It seems as if even these very commonplace items are works of art.

Although not every Swede is culturally inclined—going to the theater weekly or reading tons of books—there is little resistance to the subsidies paid to performers, writers, companies, and cultural organizations. Critics might blast a particular work, but seldom does anyone mutter that artists are receiving too much governmental support.

Probably more and more Swedes are being exposed to this "cultural revolution" as works become more widespread. Whether they will take advantage of all that is being offered is another question, one that the national commissions have been asking. Yet they still want to make those opportunities available for all Swedes, especially the young people.

So far, the programs seem to be working—and generally working well.

Education is provided by the government. Above: Students in a language laboratory. Below: A modern elementary school

Chapter 8

SWEDES AND THEIR WAYS

Sweden is going through an "educational explosion." Many more young people are continuing their schooling than ever before. A generation ago, only about 1 percent of the population went to universities. Today, more than 65 percent stay in school after their nine years of compulsory classes; 17 percent go on to college. Thousands of Swedes take adult education courses; thousands of preschoolers are in nursery schools. It seems that almost everyone is taking some sort of schooling in Sweden.

BEGINNING EDUCATION

The beginning classes are in the "comprehensive school." There pupils study many subjects rather than specialize in one field. The junior classes are grades one to three; the middle school runs from grades four to six; and the senior grades are grades seven to nine. There are two terms, one in the autumn and one in the spring.

A workshop in a training school run by an electric company.

Christmas vacation lasts three weeks and summer vacation extends from early June to late August.

Beginning in grade three, all pupils study English as a second language. In addition to science, mathematics, history, and social studies, young people have to take classes in different skills such as woodworking, textile making, and metalworking. In grades eight and nine, both boys and girls have courses in child care and home economics. At lunch time, every child gets a free hot lunch.

Senior level pupils take more difficult courses in foreign languages, geography, biology, and all the rest. They choose from many after-school activities, ranging from football (soccer) to various clubs. Often, senior level pupils go on field trips to see how people work. This helps them plan what they might like to do when they leave school.

There are many immigrant children who have come to Sweden with their parents who look for work. They are given lessons in the Swedish language. Most of the foreign children are from

An elementary school in Boras

Yugoslavia, Turkey, and West Germany. By learning Swedish ways they can make friends and lead normal lives.

More and more schools are experimenting with "teaching teams" of several teachers who work with a classroom of pupils. Since there are often twenty-five to thirty students in a classroom, this gives every child a chance to work with a teacher.

HIGHER EDUCATION

After the comprehensive school, pupils can go to the upper secondary school if they wish. Programs here run from three to four years. Courses often are geared to training for jobs; they are divided into "lines." There are three different lines in a Swedish school: one deals with arts and social subjects, another with economics and commercial subjects, and the third with science and technical subjects.

Students at Linköping University

Instead of a principal, an upper secondary school is run by a headmaster, assisted by directors of studies. All schooling for Swedish children is free.

Once in a university or professional school, Swedish students have a great deal of independence. However, there are some ways the schools make sure they take their studies seriously. Young people are entitled to a small salary from the government if they are at the university level. They get paid for studying. But students don't receive the money until a professor signs a certificate saying they are making satisfactory progress in their lessons.

All students are required to join student unions at the thirty-one institutions of higher learning in the country. Their dues are used to help run the student newspaper, provide medical and accident insurance, housing, and to arrange charter trips.

Nobel Prizes are presented yearly in the Golden Hall of Stockholm's City Hall.

SCHOLARS AND SCIENTISTS

Sweden has always been proud of its scholars. Once a year, international headlines tell about the awarding of the coveted Nobel Prizes in literature, economics, physics, chemistry, physiology or medicine, and peace.

The Royal Swedish Academy of Sciences has turned out dozens of famous personalities who have worked for the betterment of all people. Jacob Berzelius (1799-1848) and Carl Gustaf Mosander (1779-1858) discovered many chemical elements, those minute particles of matter that make up our world.

Explorers such as Sven Hedin (1865-1952) charted unknown areas of the world from central Asia to Antarctica.

Swedes have also been noted for their contributions to astronomy, medicine, the humanities, and social sciences. King Gustav VI Adolf, the grandfather of the current king of Sweden, was known for his knowledge of archaeology. Every autumn, the king would travel to Italy to spend his vacation doing research.

A busy skating rink in downtown Stockholm

SPORTS: SOCCER AND SKIING

But Swedes don't spend all their waking moments in school or doing scientific research. They also love sports. About two million Swedes belong to the Swedish Sports Federation, with soccer being the most popular game played in the country. There are about 300,000 players affiliated with clubs, in an elaborate system of senior and junior teams. More than 2,500 women play in a special league as well.

During the winter, cross-country and downhill skiing are fun. Ingemar Stenmark's championship successes in international competition in the 1980s increased the popularity of this sport.

Swedes like to keep fit. They jog, they hike, they participate in gymnastics. Even little children and older people like getting out for a walk in the woods or a cartwheel across a tumbling mat.

Björn Borg, tennis champion

The Inter-Company Athletics Association coordinates sporting events between unions and organizes sports clubs in offices and factories.

To boost participation in sports, local governments build swimming pools, lighted ice skating rinks, and playing fields. The central government has started about twenty upper secondary schools that specialize in sports, with an average enrollment of about 250. The government prefers to have athletes learn some other subjects while training, to prepare them for the time when their playing days are over. The pupils follow the usual study program, but five hours a week they can train in their favorite sport.

Other sporting events get a lot of headlines, especially when retired tennis star Björn Borg is about to serve a smash across the net. Swedish-born Borg was one of the best singles tennis players in the world.

SOCIAL PROBLEMS

Swedes like to party. There is a problem with overdrinking in Sweden, a factor that many organizations are working to correct. They are called temperance societies (there are about six thousand local chapters).

They try very hard to get people to slow down while indulging in alcohol. Alcohol abusers can find themselves on a "black list," which means they have a difficult time buying alcoholic beverages. Treatment centers always seem to be full. Motorists caught driving after they have been drinking often have to go immediately to jail, face stiff fines, and the loss of their driver's license.

Young people in Sweden are knowledgeable about sex. Their country was one of the first to have sex education in schools. These are generally fine programs that answer questions about pregnancy, marriage, and what is happening inside a growing body. Girls are quite independent, often asking boys for dates, and usually paying their own way to the movies or concerts.

HOLIDAYS OF THE SEASONS

The holidays add sparkle and spice to a Swedish year. In such a far northern country, the rhythm of the year is determined by the seasons. The dark of winter is followed by the excitement of a new spring. The sunny summer is followed by the crisp fall. Each has its own festivals, providing a chance to wear colorful costumes and to dance and sing.

New Year is considered part of the traditional Yule celebration. It is customary for hotels to sponsor New Year's Eve dances called

Sylvester Balls, where the townspeople turn out in their fanciest clothes to eat, talk, and have a good time.

At the stroke of midnight, factory sirens and ship horns honk and toot and crowds gather in the streets to celebrate. In the 1890s, a tradition started in the Skansen, an open-air museum in Stockholm, where the Tennyson poem "Ring Out, Wild Bells" is solemnly read. Today, the poem is broadcast over radio and television, but people still gather at the museum to listen to one or another of the country's most famous actors read the selection.

The day before Ash Wednesday, when Lent begins, is called Fat Tuesday. It is the climax of a round of parties and merrymaking. Sweden has never had the Mardi Gras street parades that some other countries or cities sponsor. But in the old days, horse races used to be held. Fancy dress balls are still fun to attend, however.

Anyone invited to a Swedish home on a Tuesday in the month before Easter is offered a delicious, traditional dessert: a large sweet bun floating in a bowl of warm milk. The bun has an almond filling and is topped with whipped cream.

The only saint's day that has remained since the Protestant Reformation is Annunciation Day on March 25. Sometimes the holiday, which honors the Virgin Mary, is called Lady Day.

Swedes still celebrate it because it is close to the vernal equinox, when the long winter darkness starts giving way to the light of spring. One of the customs of Lady Day is to go to sleep without a light. Supposedly by March 25 it is light enough so that country people can go to bed without a candle to brighten the way.

At Easter, little girls get to pretend they are the Easter Hag, running around the neighborhood astride broomsticks. This custom stems from pagan days, when people believed in witches.

June 6 is Swedish National Day, commemorating the date when

Drinking mead from a horn is an old Viking custom.

Gustav Vasa ascended to the throne of Sweden in 1523. It is also known as Flag Day, when the Swedish national colors are presented at parades and special ceremonies.

In middle of the year, around June 20, the Swedes celebrate Midsummer. A tall pole is decorated with green leaves and garlands of flowers are fastened to the top. The pole is lifted upright and the community dances around the decorations, singing and playing games. People stay up until sunrise.

But Christmastime remains the best of all the Swedish holidays. December 13 is called Saint Lucia Day, named after a young girl put to death during Roman times for her Christian beliefs.

Swedish children get up extra early on Saint Lucia Day morning. The girls put on long white gowns with a red ribbon around the waist. Lucia wears a crown of candles on her head; the others carry a candle. The boys wear long white shirts and pointed hats. They then make up trays with coffee and rolls and serve breakfast in bed to their parents. There are Lucia processions in school that day with all the youngsters dressed in their costumes.

This festival starts the Christmas season. A Christmas tree is decorated and presents are given on Christmas Eve. Instead of a

Midsummer Festival in Dalarna (left) and Lucia Day, December 13 (right)

Santa Claus, Swedish children wait for Father Christmas, a jolly elf who is always an easy touch for goodies—that is, if the children have been behaving all year.

When the candles on the tree have been lighted, Father Christmas bursts into the room, ho-ho-hoing and distributing presents. Usually, Father Christmas is just the family dad costumed in a long red hood, with a beard and sackful of gifts.

Christmas Day starts with a church service; the day is filled with visits and a huge meal.

The Swedes are rugged people who love their customs and their way of life. They have been molded by their land and are proud of what they have done with their country. They are eagerly looking forward to the challenges of the future. The young people of Sweden have a lot to build upon, looking back over the thousand years of their heritage. They are using those traditions and accomplishments of the past to mold a new tomorrow for themselves and for Sweden.

Cities and towns in Sweden. Lowercase letters refer to map insert on bottom right.

Abisko	C8
Åby	u34
Alberga	u34
Alingsås	I5
Alsike	t35
Älvdalen	G6
Alvsjö	t36
Åmål	H5
Ängelholm	I5
Arboga	t33
Arjeplog	D7
Arvidsjaur	E8
Arvika	H5
Åsele	E7
Askersund	H6
Åtvidaberg	H6
Avesta	G7
Bastuträsk	E9
Boden	E9
Bollnäs	G7
Borås	I5
Borensberg	u33
Borgholm	I7
Borlänge	G6
Botkyrka	t35
Burgsvik	I8
Burträsk	E9
Dalarö	t36
Degerön	u33
Djursholm	t36
Eda	H5
Eksjö	I6
Enköping	H7, t35
Eskilstuna	H7, t34
Fågelbro	t36
Fagersta	G6
Falköping	H5
Fållnäs	u35
Falun	G6
Fellingsbro	t33
Finspång	u33
Fjärdhundra	t34
Flen	t34
Gällivare	D9
Gävle	G7
Glanshammar	t33
Gnesta	t35
Göteborg	I4
Grangärde	G6
Hallsberg	t33
Hällestad	u33
Halmstad	I5
Hammarby	t35
Haparanda	E11
Härnösand	F8
Hässleholm	I5
Heby	t34
Hede	F5
Hedemora	G6
Helsingborg	I5
Hemmesta	t36
Hjo	H6
Holmsund	F9
Hoting	E7
Hudiksvall	G7
Huskvarna	I6
Järlåsa	t35
Järna	t35
Jokkmokk	D8
Jönköping	I6
Jörn	E9
Jukkasjärvi	D9
Julita	t34
Kalmar	I7, t35
Karesuando	C10
Karlshamn	I6
Karlskoga	H6
Karlskrona	I6
Karlstad	H5
Katrineholm	H7, t34
Kiruna	D9
Kolbäck	t34
Köping	H6, t34
Kristianstad	I6
Kumla	H6, t33
Kungsör	t34
Landskrona	J5
Landsort	u35
Läppe	t33
Leksand	G6
Lidingö	H8, t36
Lidköping	H5
Lindesberg	H6
Linköping	H6
Litslena	t35
Ljungby	I5
Ljusdal	G7
Ljusterö	t36
Ludvika	G6
Luleå	E10
Lund	J5
Lundby	t34
Lycksele	E8
Lysekil	H4
Malmberget	D9
Malmköping	t34
Malmö	J5
Malung	G5
Mariedamm	u33
Mariefred	t35
Mariestad	H5
Markaryd	I5
Mjölby	H6
Mölndal	I4
Mora	G6
Morjärv	D10
Motala	H6
Muskö	u36
Nässjö	I6
Nävekvarn	u34
Njurunda	F7
Nora	H6
Nordmaling	F8
Norrköping	H7, u34
Norrtälje	H8, t36
Nybro	I6
Nyköping	H7, u34
Nynäshamn	H7, u35
Ockelbo	G7
Odensala	t35
Odensbacken	t33
Örebro	H6, t33
Öregrund	G8
Örnö	t36
Örnsköldsvik	F8
Orsa	G6
Örsundsbro	t35
Oskarshamn	I7
Östanå	t36
Östersund	F6
Övertorneå	D10
Oxelösund	u35
Pajala	D10
Pålsboda	t33
Piteå	E9
Porjus	D8
Ragunda	F7
Ramnäs	t34
Rasbokil	t35
Rättvik	G6
Regna	u33
Rekarne	t34
Rimbo	t36
Sala	H7, t34
Saltsjöbaden	t36
Sandviken	G7
Särna	G5
Säter	G6
Sätrabrunn	t34
Sigtuna	t35
Simonstorp	u34
Simrishamn	J6
Skara	H5
Skellefteå	E9
Skövde	H5
Söderala	G7
Söderhamn	G7
Söderköping	H7
Södertälje	t35
Sollefteå	E9
Solna	H7
Sparreholm	t34
Stålboga	t34
Stockholm	H8, t36
Stora Sundby	t34
Storsjö	F5
Storuman	E7
Strängnäs	t35
Strängsjö	u34
Sundbyberg	t35
Sundsvall	F7
Sunne	H5
Svärtagård	u35
Sveg	F6
Tännäs	F5
Tanum	H4
Tierp	G7
Tillberga	t34
Timrå	F7
Torö	u35
Torshälla	t34
Tranås	H6
Trelleborg	J5
Trollhättan	H5
Tumba	t35
Uddevalla	H4
Ulricehamn	I5
Umeå	F9
Uppsala	H7, t35
Vagnhärad	u35
Valdemarsvik	H7
Vänersborg	H5
Varberg	I5
Värnamo	I6
Västerås	H7, t34
Västerhaninge	t36
Västervik	I7
Vaxholm	t36
Växjö	I6
Veckholm	t35
Vetlanda	I6
Vimmerby	I6
Vindeln	E8
Vingåker	t33
Virserum	I6
Visby	I8
Vrena	u34
Ystad	J5

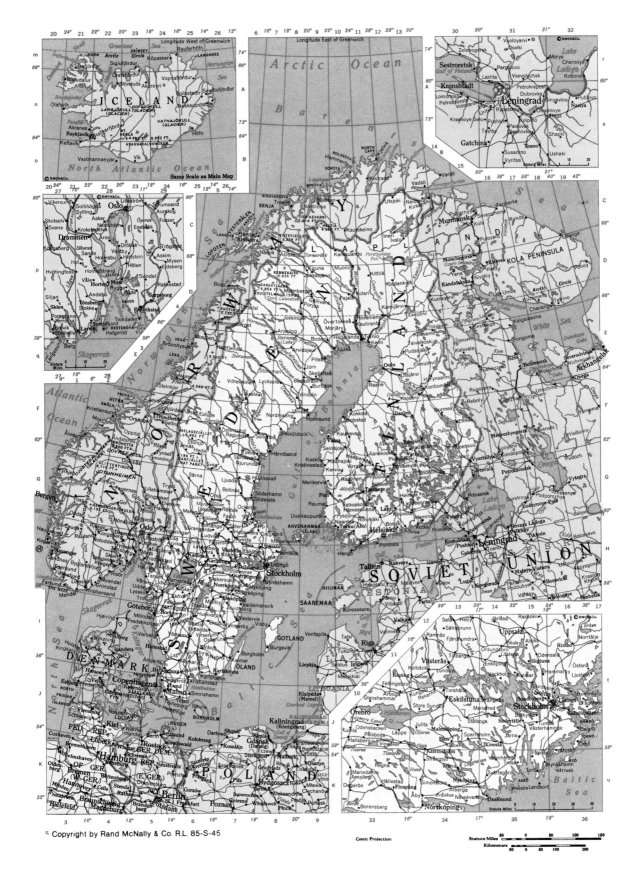

Conic Projection

Statute Miles

Kilometers

MINI-FACTS AT A GLANCE

GENERAL INFORMATION

Official Name: The Kingdom of Sweden (*Konungariket Sverige* in Swedish)

Capital: Stockholm

Official Language: Swedish

Government: Sweden is a constitutional monarchy, which means that although it has a king, Carl XVI Gustaf, it is run like a democracy. The king has only ceremonial powers, much like Queen Elizabeth of Great Britain. Like Great Britain, Sweden has a parliament, called the Riksdag. There are 349 members who serve for three-year terms. Every Swedish citizen over eighteen can vote.

There are five major parties and several minor ones. The party that gets the largest number of votes gets the most seats in the Riksdag. It can appoint the cabinet, consisting of the prime minister and seventeen ministers. The cabinet is the executive branch of government.

Sweden is divided into 25 counties and 279 municipalities. Each county is headed by a governor appointed by the national government. It also has a council elected directly by the people.

Democracy has a long history in Sweden. The Swedish Riksdag has its roots in the tribal courts (*ting*) and the election of kings in the days of the Vikings. The Swedish constitution was first written in 1809 and revised in 1866. A new version of the constitution was adopted in 1974.

Flag: The flag is believed to date from Karl Knutsson Bonde's reign during the 1400s. It is deep blue with a yellow cross.

Coat of Arms: It features three small crowns added by King Albert in 1364.

National Song: The Swedish national song is called *"Du Gamla, Du Fria."* It is based on a folk melody from Västmanland and was first sung in 1844 by Richard Dybeck.

Religion: Lutheranism is the state religion. About 95 percent of the population are Lutherans. There are a few Roman Catholics, Jews, and other types of Protestants.

Money: Money in Sweden is measured in kronor (the plural of krona). One krona is equal to 100 öre. In 1985 one krona equaled about 12 cents in United States currency.

Weights and Measures: The metric system is in use in Sweden.

Population: 8,353,000 (1985 estimate)

Cities:

Stockholm	649,686
Göteborg	425,875
Malmö	230,381
Uppsala	149,300
Norrköping	118,236
Västerås	117,793
Örebro	117,367

(Population figures based on 1982 estimate)

GEOGRAPHY

Highest Point: Mount Kebnekaise, 6,926 ft. (2,111 m)

Lowest Point: Sea level

Coastline: 4,700 mi. (7,564 km)

Lakes: There are approximately 96,000 lakes in Sweden. The largest is Lake Vänern, covering 2,156 sq. mi. (5,584 km²).

Climate: The Swedish climate is affected by the North Atlantic Drift, the ocean current that sweeps up the Atlantic. If it weren't for these warm waters, agriculture couldn't thrive this far north. The weather in the north is very different from the south. In the far north at Karesuando the mean February temperature is 7° F. (-14° C), and at Lund in the far south it is 30° F. (-1° C). July mean temperatures at the same cities are 57° F. (14° C) at Karesuando and 63° F. (17° C) at Lund.

Northern Sweden is called the Land of the Midnight Sun. One seventh of Sweden is north of the Arctic Circle. Here, the sun never sets for several weeks in June and July and it never really gets dark for weeks throughout the summer. On the other hand, in winter, the sun never rises north of the circle.

Greatest Distances: North to south—977 mi. (1,572 km)
East to west—310 mi. (499 km)

Area: 173,732 sq. mi. (499,964 km²)

NATURE

Vegetation: In the alpine or mountainous regions, mostly mosses and lichens grow in the highest elevations. There are also dwarf birches, rowans, bird cherries, willows, and aspens. In the north and central parts of Sweden, Scotch pines, spruce, lowland birches, rowans, and aspens grow. Oaks, ashes, lindens, maples, and elms are found in the south. Beech trees are found in Skåne.

Fish: Salmon, trout, char, pike, and perch are found in rivers and lakes. Shrimp, herring, cod, flatfish, mackerel, and sprat are found in the ocean.

Animals: Bears and lynx are found in northern forests. Herds of reindeer are found in northern mountains. Älg (moose) is found throughout Sweden. There are also badgers, foxes, hare, otters, and roe deer. The wolf, which is almost extinct, is protected by the Swedish government.

Birds: There are numerous species of birds, including songbirds, game birds, forest birds of prey, cranes, gulls, terns, and eider ducks.

EVERYDAY LIFE

Food: Swedes love fine cooking. They especially enjoy the "natural" ways of preparing food, without all sorts of sauces and spices to cover the real flavor of food. They love fruits and vegetables—apples, pears, raspberries, blueberries, wild strawberries, mushrooms, lingonberries, and cloudberries.

Sweden's gift to the world is the smörgåsbord, which is a large buffet. It often consists of herring, boiled potatoes, smoked eel, jellied fish, roast beef, tongue, and cheese. Among the best known cheeses are Västerbottensost from the Norrland, Prästost from Småland, and Herrgårdsost—which can be found everywhere. A great addition to crayfish or shrimp is Kryddost, a cheese spiced with caraway and cloves.

Holidays:

January 1, New Year's Day
January 6, Epiphany
Good Friday
Easter Monday
May 1, May Day
May 31, Ascension Day
Whit Monday
June 23, Midsummer
November 3, All Souls' Day
December 25-26, Christmas

Culture: The arts are very important in Swedish life. In fact, the government subsidizes cultural activities. The Swedish National Council for Cultural Affairs oversees government contributions to theater, dance, music, literature, public libraries, cultural magazines, visual arts, museums, and exhibitions.

Children's books have always been important in Sweden. A magazine for young people was started in 1785. Folktales collected by Gunnar Olof Hyltén-Cavallius in the mid-1800s are still in print today. Astrid Lindgren is world famous for her *Pippi Longstocking* books. Other children's writers include Gunnel Beckman, Inger Brattström, Maria Gripe, and Rose Lagercrantz.

Children are also familiar with theater in Sweden. "Visiting Theater" gives performances on playgrounds, in nursery schools, or almost anywhere children gather.

The movie industry is very important in Sweden. Director Ingmar Bergman and stars Max Von Sydow, Ingrid Bergman, and Bibi Andersson are famous all over the world. Swedish producers like series of movies that deal with the same characters.

In the visual arts, the Swedes are noted for design of all sorts. For example, Carl Milles is a very famous sculptor; Sigurd Persson is well known for jewelry. Architecture, furniture, textiles, and glass are other areas in which Swedes excel.

Sports and Recreation: Swedes love sports. About two million Swedes belong to the Swedish Sports Federation. Soccer is the most popular game played in the country. But during winter, cross-country and downhill skiing are very popular.

Local governments also sponsor athletic activities. For example, they build swimming pools, lighted ice-skating rinks, and playing fields. The central government has recently started secondary schools that specialize in sports.

Communication: There are about 150 newspapers in Sweden, many affiliated with a political party. Many papers are owned by political parties or by trade unions. The major daily newspapers in Stockholm are *Expressen, Dagens Nyheter, Aftonbladet,* and *Svenska Dagbladet.*

There are probably three thousand or more periodicals (magazines) published in the country, also.

The Swedish Broadcasting Company directs the broadcast industry. There are three radio channels and two national television networks.

Transportation: There are over 7,000 mi. (11,265 km) of nationalized railroads. Ferries go to Denmark and the German Democratic Republic. There are more than 80,000 mi. (127,747 km) of roads. Buses, trains, subways, and taxis are available in cities. Major airlines serve Stockholm and Göteborg.

Shipping on the seas as well as lakes and canals has always been important. From Swedish ports, goods are shipped to other countries. Traffic on the inland waters is a lot less important than it was historically.

Schools: All children must attend school, beginning at age seven, for nine years. The nine-year program is called comprehensive school, which is divided into three parts: lower, middle, and upper. All children study the same things for the first six years. Beginning in the seventh year, students choose different curricula. About 30 percent of the students choose courses that will prepare them for the university.

The Swedish system emphasizes foreign languages. English is the first foreign language that pupils are taught. Later, in the upper grades, they can study German, French, Russian, Spanish, Finnish, or Italian.

There are six universities: in Stockholm, Linköping, Göteborg, Uppsala, Lund, and Umeå. Other schools offer education in medicine, art, music, journalism, and technology.

Health: The Swedish social welfare system is very far reaching. Money spent on social services such as health care takes a great deal of the taxpayer's money. As a result, health statistics reflect the high degree of health care available to the average Swede. For example, there are many hospital beds for the number of people in the country, about 16.4 for every 1,000 people.

Housing: Most Swedes live in comfortable housing. However, many Swedes live in more crowded areas. About one third of all Swedes live in and around the three biggest cities. Fewer than half of Sweden's citizens live in individual houses.

Principal Products:
Agriculture: Barley, oats, potatoes, rye, sugar beets, wheat, livestock (cattle, hogs), milk and other dairy products
Manufacturing: Agricultural machinery, aircraft, automobiles, ball bearings, diesel motors, electrical equipment, explosives, fertilizers, furniture, glass, matches, paper and cardboard, plastics, plywood, textiles, and telephones
Minerals: Copper, gold, iron ore, lead, uranium, and zinc

IMPORTANT DATES

862—Rurik, a Swede, founds Novgorod, one of the earliest Russian cities of any importance

late 800s—Saint Ansgar tries to introduce Christianity to the Swedes

1160—Eric IX is assassinated by a disgruntled Danish prince

1319—Sweden and Norway are united by Magnus VII

1362 — Finland becomes a Swedish province

1397 — Kalmar Union unites Danes, Finns, Norwegians, and Swedes under a common crown

1435 — Arboga assembly established, first Riksdag (parliament) in Swedish history

1477 — University of Uppsala founded

1520 — Christian II, king of Denmark, massacres Swedish nobles; incident becomes known as Stockholm Bloodbath

1523 — Gustav Vasa becomes first hereditary Swedish monarch

1556 — Finland made a grand duchy of Sweden

1618-1648 — Thirty Years War

1621 — Gothenburg (Göteborg) is founded

1632 — Gustavus Adolphus killed at the Battle of Lutzen

1697 — Charles XII becomes king

1709 — Swedes are defeated by the Russians

1718-1773 — Sweden's "Age of Freedom"

1741-1743 — War between Russia and Sweden, resulting in cession of part of Finland to Russia

1788-1790 — War between Russia and Sweden

1809 — Russia annexes Finland; first Swedish constitution adopted; Norway becomes Swedish territory

1842 — Riksdag introduces compulsory education

1866 — Constitution revised

1880s — Many Swedes immigrate to the United States

1905 — Norway becomes independent of Sweden

1913—First national pension plan goes into effect

1914—World War I begins; Sweden remains neutral

1917—Sweden adopts parliamentary type of government

1921—Universal suffrage introduced (all citizens over eighteen can vote)

1931—Regional and local health insurance programs introduced

1939—World War II begins; Sweden remains neutral

1955—Employees legally guaranteed vacations with pay and women granted maternity leave with pay

1971—Riksdag becomes a one-house assembly

1973—Carl XVI Gustav becomes king

1974—Constitution revised

1976—Social Democrats defeated after forty-four years in power; the Center party and other non-Socialists take over

1980—Act of Succession

1982—Social Democrats are returned to power; Swedes chase Soviet submarines away from their military bases

1986—Prime Minister Olof Palme assassinated; succeeded by Ingvar Carlsson

IMPORTANT PEOPLE

Kristina Ahlmark-Michanek, author, proponent of women's rights
Saint Ansgar (801-865), Frankish missionary who tried to introduce Christianity to Scandinavia
Ingmar Bergman (1918-   ), movie director, writer, and producer
Ingrid Bergman (1915-1982), actress

Count Folke Bernadotte (1895-1948), saved thousands of people from Nazi concentration camps during World War II; chairman of the Swedish Red Cross from 1943 to 1948; chief United Nations mediator in Palestine (1948)

Jöns Jakob Berzelius (1779-1848), scientist

Jussi Björling (1911-1960), operatic tenor

Björn Borg (1956-   ), tennis world champion

Fredrika Bremer (1801-1865), novelist, champion of women's rights

Carl XVI Gustav (1946-   ), current king of Sweden

Carl Philip (1979-   ), prince, son of current king

Charles XII (1682-1718), king of Sweden from 1697 to 1718

Charles XIII (1748-1818), king of Sweden from 1809-1818

Charles XIV Johan (1763-1844), king of Sweden from 1818 to 1844; founder of current Swedish dynasty; was called Jean Baptiste Bernadotte before he became king

Christian II (1481-1559), king of Denmark and Norway from 1513 to 1523 and Sweden from 1520 to 1523

John Ericsson (1803-1889), Swedish-born American engineer who built the *Monitor* ship, used in the American Civil War

Eric IX (?-1160), king from 1150 to 1160; patron saint of Sweden

Greta Garbo (1905-   ), American actress born in Sweden

Gustav Eriksson Vasa (Gustavus I) (1496?-1560), first hereditary monarch of Sweden

Gustav III (1746-1792), king of Sweden from 1771 to 1792 during Sweden's "Golden Age"

Gustavus Adolphus (Gustavus II) (1594-1632), king of Sweden from 1611 to 1632; killed at the Battle of Lutzen

Roland Haeberlein, sculptor

Dag Hammarskjöld (1905-1961), statesman, secretary general of the United Nations from 1953 to 1961

Sven Hedin (1865-1952), explorer, geographer, and writer

Olle Hellbom (1925-1982), movie producer and director

Gunnar Olof Hyltén-Cavallius (1818-1889), compiler of folktales

Ellen Key (1849-1926), author and champion of women's rights

Pär F. Lagerkvist (1891-1974), novelist, playwright, and poet

Selma Lagerlöf (1858-1940), novelist

Jenny Lind (1820-1887), famous soprano, called the "Swedish Nightingale"

Carl von Linné (1707-1778), botanist

Madeleine (1982-   ), princess, daughter of current king

Magnus VII (1316-1374), king of Norway and Sweden

Margaret of Denmark (1353-1412), queen of Denmark, Norway, and Sweden

Carl Milles (1875-1955), sculptor

Vilhelm Moberg (1898-1973), novelist, author of *The Emigrants*

Carl Gustaf Mosander (1779-1858), chemist

Alva Myrdal (1902-1986), cabinet minister from 1967 to 1973; proponent of military disarmament

Gunnar Myrdal (1898-   ), Nobel Prize winner in economics in 1974

Birgit Nilsson (1911-   ), operatic soprano

Alfred Nobel (1833-1896), manufacturer, philanthropist, and inventor of dynamite; bequeathed funds to establish Nobel Prizes

Olle Nordemar, movie producer

Nils A. Nordenskjöld (1832-1901), geologist and explorer

Alex G. Oxenstierna (1583-1654), statesman

Göran Palm (1931-   ) writer

Sigurd Persson (1914-   ), jeweler

Kaj Pollack (1938-   ), screen writer and movie director

Alexander Roslin (1718-1793), portrait painter

Rurik (?-879), founder of Novgorod, one of the first important cities in Russia

Carl Wilhelm Scheele (1742-1786), pharmacist and chemist; discovered oxygen and other elements

Karl M.G. Siegbahn (1886-1978), awarded Nobel Prize in physics in 1924

Silvia (1943-   ), current queen of Sweden

August Strindberg (1849-1912), playwright and novelist

Arne Suckdorff (1917-   ), movie producer

Theodor Svedberg (1884-1971), awarded Nobel Prize in chemistry in 1926

Cornelius Tacitus (55?-117?), Roman historian who wrote about Germanic tribes who were ancestors of the modern Swedes

Victoria (1977-   ), crown princess, daughter of current king

Max Von Sydow (1929-   ), actor

Sven Wernström (1925-   ), playwright

Siv Widerberg (1931-   ), novelist and poet

Anders Zorn (1860-1920), painter, etcher, and sculptor

INDEX

Page numbers that appear in boldface type indicate illustrations

About the Author

Martin Hintz, a former newspaper reporter, has written more than a dozen books for young people. The subjects range from training elephants to other social studies titles included in the Childrens Press Enchantment of the World series. He and his family currently live in Milwaukee, Wisconsin. Hintz has a master's degree in journalism and is a professional travel writer/photographer who has won numerous awards for his work.

Special thanks in preparing *Sweden* are extended to Claes Sweger, director of information for the Swedish Information Service; Eva Hedencrona of the Swedish Consulate General staff; Ed Conradsen of the Swedish National Tourist Office; Frederic Fleisher; Donald Connery; Scandinavian Airlines; the Lilla Sällskapet Gastronomic Society; and the Swedish Institute.